THE AUSTRALIAN AIR CAMPAIGN SERIES – 11

FROM THE SKIES

Australian air power in humanitarian aid and disaster relief since the Second World War

Karyn Markwell

Disclaimer
This book provides a representation of Australian air power (both Australian Defence Force and commercial) in humanitarian aid and disaster relief throughout history. It is not intended to be an exhaustive reference to this topic; this would require many, much larger volumes.

All quotes and narratives provided are personal opinions and recollections and do not necessarily reflect the views of the author, the Royal Australian Air Force or the Australian Defence Force.

While great care has been taken to ensure the accuracy of all information, neither the author nor the Royal Australian Air Force nor the Australian Defence Force accept responsibility for any errors, omissions or misrepresentations.

All inquiries should be made to the publishers.
Big Sky Publishing Pty Ltd
PO Box 303, Newport, NSW 2106, Australia
Phone: 1300 364 611
Email: info@bigskypublishing.com.au
Web: www.bigskypublishing.com.au

Series: Australian Air Campaign Series; 11

A catalogue record for this book is available from the National Library of Australia

Cover design and typesetting by Think Productions, Melbourne

Front cover and title page: Australian Army personnel boarding a Royal Australian Air Force C-130J Hercules bound for Melbourne prior to serving during Operation *COVID-19 Assist* in 2020 (Defence)

Back cover images:

- (Main) An Australian Army MRH-90 Taipan launching from the flight deck of HMAS *Adelaide* to deliver relief supplies to the island of Vanua Levu in Fiji during Operation *Fiji Assist 2020* (Defence)
- (Insert, top) Royal Australian Air Force personnel caring for Vietnamese orphans of war during Operation *Babylift* in 1975 (Defence)
- (Inset, middle) A Royal Australian Air Force loadmaster high-fives a young passenger during an evacuation flight in 2023 following Ex-Tropical Cyclone *Ellie* (Defence)
- (Insert, bottom) Queensland Search and Rescue dogs and their handlers preparing to depart for Japan via a RAAF C-17 during Operation *Pacific Assist 2011* (Defence)

CONTENTS

'[He] rides the heavens to help you, and in His excellency on the clouds'
Deuteronomy 33:26

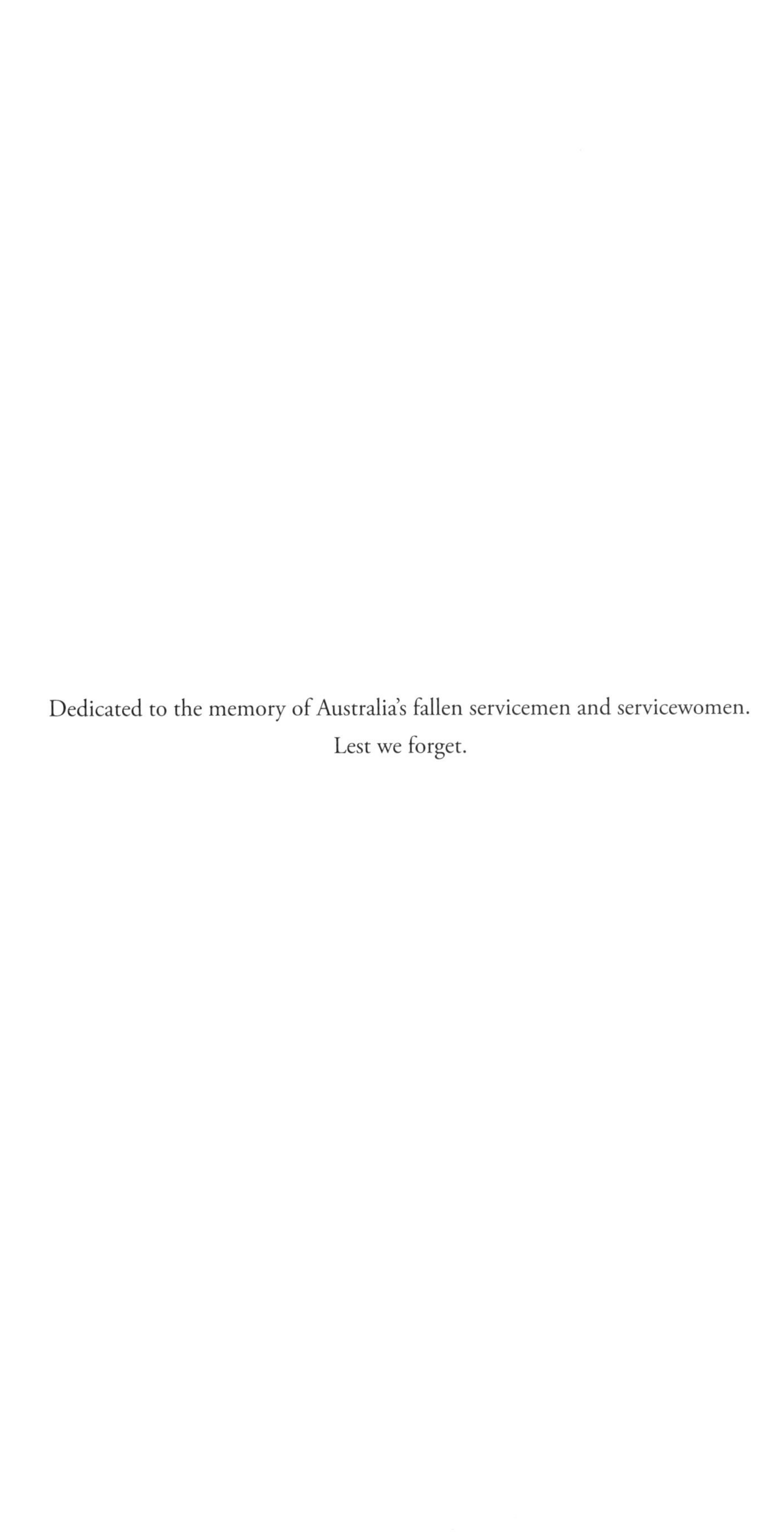

Dedicated to the memory of Australia's fallen servicemen and servicewomen.

Lest we forget.

SERIES FOREWORD

The Australian Air Campaign Series produced by History and Heritage – Air Force focuses on four themed sub-series:

- campaigns, operations and battles
- capability and technology
- bases and airfields
- people.

These themed titles explore specific facets of the Air Force from its inception in 1921. What they reveal are unique insights, providing the reader with a greater appreciation and deeper understanding of those aspects that have shaped the Air Force's history and heritage.

Importantly, these publications are sourced from official records and research, often including first-hand accounts. While endorsed for studies in military history, the range of topics in these publications provides an ideal conduit for the broadest of audiences to pursue and learn more about the many aspects that have contributed to the development of Australia's Air Force.

Apart from being a significant point of reference, these publications ultimately acknowledge bravery, ingenuity and resilience – in essence, the service and sacrifice which is the hallmark of those who have served and continue to serve in the Air Force.

Robert Lawson, OAM
Air Commodore
Director-General History and Heritage – Air Force

FOREWORD

In my previous life as a doctor in the Royal Australian Air Force, I was often asked how I reconciled my Hippocratic oath with belonging to an organisation whose role was to kill people! My response was to patiently explain that there is no greater mission or purpose in life than serving one's country and its people, and that I was proud to be part of an organisation whose job was security, not just against 'hard threats and hard power', but also in helping to make safe those in need; in other words, by also supporting human security.

Impacts on human security can result from many causes – wars, pandemics, famines, natural disasters, incidents at sea, etc – and take many forms. The Australian Defence Force (ADF) and the broader nation have the skills to help, and responding and employing these skills in times of crisis is one of the highest callings for ADF personnel. And sometimes we even put ourselves in harm's way to aid the greater good.

In fact, while Australia has engaged in several wars since the Second World War, it has had an even bigger role in ensuring or re-establishing human security, including through the provision of humanitarian aid and disaster relief (HADR). The purpose of these missions has not only been to ensure that Australians are kept safe wherever they roam, but just as often are directed towards people of other nations whose need is great. In the latter instance, our role in improving human security often has second- and third-order effects by improving regional or broader security aims through the exercise of soft power.

But what is sometimes forgotten is that it takes a team to produce this effect. While sometimes it may look like the personnel on the ground are the heroes (for example, aeromedical-evacuation personnel at an airport), they can only do this with an entire team: from logisticians to operations staff, from health personnel to aircrew. Australian aircraft, including those of the ADF, have played a crucial role in ensuring that human security can be preserved throughout our country and globally as part of a whole-of-ADF effort.

This book looks at why Australia engages in HADR, what we have done during the past 80 years and why the role of the ADF is so important. It covers a wide scope of missions, including delivering relief supplies, aeromedical evacuation, search-and-rescue and damage-assessment missions, repatriation missions and delivering personnel to where the need is greatest. It does this through the unique lens of how aircraft – both military and commercial – have been used and argues that this role is an essential part of air power. In doing so, it reinforces the importance of the ADF's role in keeping people safe, wherever and whoever they might be.

Tracy Smart, AO
Air Vice-Marshal (retd)
Former surgeon general of the ADF

PROLOGUE

Wednesday 7 May 1997
South Pacific Ocean

Abandoning a man drifting alone on a raft in the South Pacific Ocean at night did not sit easily with Squadron Leader Tony McCormack. But as the tactical coordinator (TACCO) of the Royal Australian Air Force (RAAF) Lockheed P-3C Orion circling high above the raft, he had no choice. He had the safety of his aircrew to consider.

The previous several hours had been filled with activity and suspense for Squadron Leader McCormack and the crew of Orion A9-664. A German aviator named Horst Ellenberger had been forced to ditch his Beechcraft V35 Bonanza in the South Pacific Ocean the previous day. After being tasked to search for Horst, the Orion and its crew had left their previous overnight stop in the Solomon Islands, an archipelago almost 2,000 kilometres from mainland Australia. Their destination: the coordinates where the Rescue Coordination Centre in Canberra had calculated a raft deployed from the Bonanza would have drifted, based on time, wind and currents.

As the Orion approached the coordinates and started to descend beneath the clouds, those crewmembers who were seated by a window carefully scanned the endless blue ocean for a glimpse of a raft.

There was no sign of it.

The Orion's pilot and aircraft captain, Lieutenant Smith, an officer on exchange from the United States Navy, made ever-widening circles as all available crewmembers continued to scan the ocean. McCormack only tore his gaze from his nearest window to operate the radio, calling each of the emergency frequencies in turn.

'All stations, all stations, this is AUSY 130, AUSY 130, a Royal Australian Air Force Orion aircraft on a search-and-rescue mission; is anyone receiving this transmission?'

Silence. He repeated the call.

'Can anyone hear this transmission?'

Silence.

Finally, a burst of crackle on the VHF emergency frequency 121.5 MHz.

'Mayday, mayday, mayday!' – the internationally recognised call of distress.

'Please come back!' Horst Ellenberger cried. 'You have just flown past me, a pilot in a life raft. Mayday, mayday, mayday!'

Being able to talk to Horst was a crucial first step – and importantly, now they had made contact with him, the Orion's onboard electronic systems could home exactly onto his location.

'We've fixed the position!' called the sensor employment manager.

While Lieutenant Smith redirected the Orion to the new coordinates, all available eyes continued to scan the ocean for the raft. Many of the aircrew swapped positions so those with fresh eyes could have their turn at a window.

One crewmember suddenly cried out: 'Mark, mark, mark, life raft visual, passing under the port wing!'

A tiny splash of orange in the midst of blue – and it was gone.

'Roger, contact has been marked in the computer, smoke deployed!'

'Copied, returning to the datum!' called the captain.

The aircrew continued to scan the ocean as Smith circled the area.

'Mark, mark, mark, life raft visual!' cried several crewmembers all at once.

'We have you visual,' McCormack radioed Horst. 'We're going to drop some sonobuoys around you. Then we'll always know exactly where you are.'

There was a flurry of activity as the Orion dropped a series of sonobuoys in a large circle around the life raft. Meanwhile, McCormack checked that Horst was unhurt after his crash and more than 24 hours drifting in the raft.

'I am unharmed,' said Horst. 'I braced my shoulder against the cabin wall when I was about to hit the water.'

'Do you have food and water?'

'Yes, I have a survival canister.'

The Rescue Coordination Centre advised the Orion aircrew that the patrol boat RMIS *Lomor* from the Marshall Islands was en route to the location, having left its port the day earlier, only three hours after Horst had ditched. But the ship was still several hours away. Squadron Leader McCormack gave the order to his crew to investigate if any other ships were closer.

'None of our ships are in the vicinity, TACCO,' one crewmember told McCormack after a while, referring to the Royal Australian Navy.

More radio calls, more frequencies to try, more questions to ask.

'What's that trawler down there?' asked the squadron leader sometime later. 'They must be the closest.'

'They're not responding, TACCO.'

McCormack got back on the radio to Horst.

'The RMIS *Lomor* is on its way to pick you up,' he said. 'But it's still several hours away, so you'll need to be patient. Do you know how much battery power you have left in your radio?'

'I am not sure ...'

'Okay. Here's what we need you to do. Are you wearing a watch? You need to turn off your radio. In exactly 30 minutes, you can turn it back on. We'll have a chat, see how you are. Then you'll need to turn it off again. We'll keep doing that every 30 minutes until the *Lomor* gets here. Do you understand?'

Horst may have been forced to wait patiently – adrift in a featureless ocean with only a circle of sonobuoys around him and the drone of an aircraft far above to remind him he was not alone – but the Orion crew were busy. The two flight engineers on board calculated that the Orion did not have enough fuel to last until the patrol boat arrived. Even worse, the sun was rapidly sinking towards the ocean, which meant the Orion would no longer be able to land at the nearest airfield – in the island nation of Kiribati – which could only be used during daylight hours. Instead, they would have to fly further to the island of Nauru, an additional 700 kilometres away.

'Captain, this is TACCO, we need to conserve fuel,' McCormack spoke to the flight deck via headset.

'Roger, TACCO; we'll climb to 5,000 feet and then shut down the outboard engines.'

'Copied,' said McCormack. 'Eng, Nav, can you work out a bingo time for me? I want to know how long we can stay on station.'[1]

'Roger, TACCO.'

The blue ocean turned to indigo and then finally to black as the crew of AUSY 130 continued its working vigil high above Horst in the raft. Their duties were many. Squadron Leader McCormack, as TACCO, was in overall charge of the rescue operation while keeping up Horst's spirits during their regular, but short, radio calls. Lieutenant Smith and his two co-pilots focused on safely flying the aircraft while maintaining radio contact with the nearest air traffic control centre, located in Fiji. The sensor employment manager ensured all the Orion's electronic and visual sensors were working to their highest capabilities. The navigator–communicator was especially busy, monitoring the positions of both the survivor and the Orion, providing regular reports to the RAAF and Rescue Coordination Centre back in Australia, while monitoring weather updates and the status of the airfield in Nauru. The two flight engineers ensured the Orion's systems were all operating effectively, and constantly recalculated the fuel usage to ensure they would have enough to safely make it to Nauru later that night. The half-dozen sensor operators rotated between manning the aircraft's electronic sensor systems and its visual-search stations – another term for windows.

Through the long hours, crewmembers who were not on critical tasks delivered water, juice, tea and coffee to their colleagues throughout the aircraft to keep everyone hydrated and alert. When rumbling stomachs indicated it was well past dinnertime, they distributed sandwiches and 'Frozos' – frozen dinners heated in the small onboard oven – throughout the aircraft.

It was now fully dark and an hour before RMIS *Lomor* was due to arrive at the life raft. But McCormack had some hard news to tell Horst. With a heavy heart, he picked up the radio receiver for his final call.

'The *Lomor* is approaching from the north; can you see her lights?' he asked. 'It will be with you in an hour. But we need to leave you now. We have only just enough fuel left to make it to Nauru.'

The radio burst into life with both a string of heartfelt thanks and a touch of panic. Horst might be able to see the ship, but how would the ship be able to see him?

'As we go, we're going to drop a line of smoke marker buoys between you and the *Lomor*,' said Squadron Leader McCormack. 'That'll help them find you.'

'Even in the dark?'

'Even in the dark. The *Lomor* is heading directly for you; they'll be able to see the flames straight away. Then they'll see the smoke as they get closer.'

'But wait!' Horst cried. 'Let me give you some information about myself so you can tell the *Lomor*.'

'There's no need,' said McCormack. 'We know everything about you. At the moment, you're the most important person in the Pacific!'

Lieutenant Smith restarted the two engines he had shut down many hours earlier, and descended so the aircrew could just make out the raft on the black sea, still bobbing inside its circle of sonobuoys. As they departed, McCormack gave the order to the sensor operators to deploy a number of long-life smoke markers by hand through a free-fall chute.

A brief rainfall of buoys in the night sky, then sudden splashes and bursts of bright flames and wreaths of grey smoke.

'Goodbye and good luck,' Tony McCormack said to Horst Ellenberger. 'We've told the *Lomor* to follow the line of smoke straight to you. You just need to wait for a few more minutes ...'[2]

INTRODUCTION

This book explores the role of Australian air power in humanitarian aid and disaster relief (HADR) since the Second World War (1939–45). That is, how Australia has used (and continues to use) aircraft to aid those in need following disasters, both overseas and within its own borders.

Due to Australia's geographical location and immense size, Australians have embraced aviation since the earliest days of the technology as a way to overcome the tyranny of distance. Australia has a long and rich history of aviation pioneering and achievements, including being one of the first nations to establish long-distance air travel and regular airmail services, and many of the nation's most cherished citizens and entities – such as Sir Charles Kingsford Smith and the Royal Flying Doctor Service – have explored the full potentials of aviation and how it can be used to benefit humankind.

A global overview of humanitarian aid and disaster relief

HADR involves providing assistance to people who have been affected by a disaster or humanitarian crisis. The United Nations defines HADR as aid provided to an affected population that complies with the basic humanitarian principles of humanity, impartiality and neutrality, with the aim of saving lives, limiting suffering and preventing further damage to the affected society.[1] The disaster may be a natural one, such as an earthquake or cyclone; a manmade one, such as war or a terrorist attack; or a combination of the two, such as occurred when an earthquake and tsunami in Japan in 2011 triggered the subsequent meltdown of the Fukushima Daiichi Nuclear Power Plant. In this case, the earthquake and tsunami were natural events, but the scale of the disaster – and the number of lives lost – was greatly magnified by the presence of the nuclear power plant.

HADR dates to antiquity. Historically, empires and nations provided HADR to peoples they had conquered to win their loyalty or to convert a population to a particular faith or belief system. Only since relatively recently in history – within the past 400 years with the Age of Enlightenment – have the motivations for engaging in HADR expanded to include altruistic motivations: people genuinely wanting to help other people.[2] Today, many countries engage in HADR predominantly for altruistic reasons. They regard it as their duty as members of the human race to help others who are in need.

But a secondary motivation is to safeguard or promote their own country's strategic national interests. After all, if one's neighbours are suffering from a natural or manmade disaster, the effects can spill over into one's own country, for example, through the spread of disease or the arrival of more refugees than can be practically assisted. This desire to protect national and political interests is the reason why many governments will frequently send one of their best-equipped and best-trained assets – their military – to provide HADR beyond their own borders. They do this despite warnings from various authorities – including the Office for the Coordination of Humanitarian Affairs (OCHA) and the North Atlantic Treaty Organization (NATO) – that a nation which has experienced a disaster should request the assistance of foreign militaries only when no comparable civilian alternatives are available.[3]

How this book is structured

Despite the nation's extensive contributions to HADR, no in-depth appreciation of the use of Australian air power in HADR operations has yet been conducted. This book is the starting point of this appreciation and explores the extensive, multifaceted and professional nature of Australian airborne HADR operations across eight decades. It is a story of people, of Australia's engagement with the world, and of the skill and discipline of our aviators.

This book consists of three parts.

Part I provides the historical and socio-political context for HADR. It investigates the various reasons why empires and nations engaged in HADR throughout history, then compares the historical record with the various reasons why nations – including Australia – engage in HADR today.

Part II explores the different air-power tactics the Australian Defence Force (ADF) and Australian commercial airlines have used to provide HADR since the Second World War, right up to the present day. It demonstrates all three ADF services – the Royal Australian Navy (RAN), the Australian Army and the Royal Australian Air Force (RAAF) – provide Australia's military aviation HADR capability, while Australia's flagship airline, Qantas, has historically been the predominant HADR provider among Australia's commercial airlines. It is worthwhile pausing here to note the inclusion of the RAN and Army in a book about air power is not incongruous: these services operate the ADF's helicopter fleets and can also support the RAAF's provision of air power.

Finally, Part III of this book explores why Australia is likely to continue to engage in HADR in the future and why air power will almost certainly be a key enabler of Australia's future HADR efforts. It touches on historical precedents before exploring current trends and the new and emerging aviation technologies which Australia may use in its future HADR missions, including advanced intelligence, surveillance and reconnaissance capabilities.

HADR and the application of air power is about people. To best bring to life the use of Australian air power in HADR missions, this book features firsthand stories by members of the ADF:

Delivery and airdrop of relief supplies

- Flying Officer Jorge Elosegui Guerra (RAAF): Operation *Tonga Assist 2022*
- Air Commodore Tony McCormack (RAAF): Operation *Pacific Assist 2011* (Japan)
- Captain Jace Hutchison (RAN): Operation *Vanuatu Assist 2023*

- Wing Commander Stuart Wheal (RAAF): COVID-19 support during Operation *Lilia* (Solomon Islands, 2022)
- Leading Aircraftman Sam Schmidt (RAAF): COVID-19 support during Operation *Lilia* (Solomon Islands, 2022)
- Warrant Officer Shaunn Segon (RAAF): Ex-Tropical Cyclone *Ellie* (Western Australia, 2023)

Evacuation and aeromedical evacuation

- Squadron Leader Kevin Auld (RAAF): Operation *Ramp* (Lebanon, 2006)
- Sergeant Jacquelyn Nelson (RAAF): Operation *Carnelian* (Sudan, 2023)
- Corporal Deniele Oehm (RAAF): Ex-Tropical Cyclone *Ellie* (Western Australia, 2023)

Aerial search and rescue, aerial damage assessment and repatriation of bodies via air

- Air Commodore Tony McCormack (RAAF): missing German aviator (South Pacific Ocean, 1997)
- Group Captain Roger McCutcheon (RAAF): 1996–97 Vendée Globe around-the-world yacht race (Southern Ocean)
- Air Commodore Craig Heap (RAAF): Operation *Southern Indian Ocean*, 2014
- Flight Lieutenant Cale Barnes (RAAF): Operation *Southern Indian Ocean*, 2014

Transporting personnel to provide humanitarian aid and disaster relief

- Squadron Leader Cameron Brockel (RAAF): Operation *COVID-19 Assist* (Tasmania, 2020)
- Petty Officer Scott Broughton (RAN): Operation *Ashika Assist* (Tonga, 2009)
- Colonel Phil Baldoni (Army): quarantine of Australians from Wuhan (Christmas Island, 2020)
- Squadron Leader David Weekley (RAAF): quarantine of Australians from Wuhan (Christmas Island, 2020)

These stories are accounts by Australian men and women who helped to save lives, search for survivors, repatriate the bodies of their fellow Australians, and prevent disasters from becoming even greater. All are told in their own words with professional insight, great sensitivity and an awareness that they were privileged to help others on behalf of Australia and the ADF.

Their first-hand accounts highlight a couple of key themes. Firstly, Australia has an enduring involvement in the provision of HADR from the air. This is regulated and well framed in long-established governance standards. Secondly, Australian HADR operations are extensive in range and nature.

An Australian overview of humanitarian aid and disaster relief

Australia engages in HADR for both altruistic and strategic national and political reasons. Similar to many other nations, Australia's military plays a large role in providing HADR, both domestically as well as internationally, despite cautions by OCHA, NATO and other authorities. The ADF's *Campaigns and Operations* doctrine asserts the ADF only becomes involved in international HADR upon request by a nation in need:

> DFAT [Australia's Department of Foreign Affairs and Trade], or the head of mission in country, is responsible for confirming the host nation's declaration of a foreign disaster or situation that requires a response.[4]

The ADF's *Stabilisation and Humanitarian Operations* doctrine confirms its HADR efforts are respectful and appropriate:

> The Australian Defence Force provides humanitarian assistance and disaster relief, and humanitarian intervention, as part of a whole-of-government response to a host nation … [these] activities respect the sovereignty of a host nation.[5]

The ADF's extensive logistical capabilities and resources mean it is often well positioned to support requests for HADR.[6] In fact, the ADF is one of the few Australian institutions or organisations capable of responding – and responding quickly – to major disasters:[7]

> The ADF has to be, and is, a flexible and mobile force with sufficient levels of readiness and sustainability to achieve outcomes in relief operations. The skills and the capabilities that we need to deploy to sustain our forces for war fighting are fundamentally very similar to those required for humanitarian relief; so we can and do easily adapt our war-fighting force for these types of operations.[8]

But just because the ADF *can* engage in HADR, does it necessarily follow that it *should*? A broader question is: why should Australia engage in HADR – especially internationally – at all? Why should the Australian Government spend billions of dollars to help others? In particular, why should it risk the lives of its own citizens by sending them into foreign disaster locations or warzones?

Australia engages in HADR predominantly due to its identity as a responsible and caring global citizen. The Australian Government knows providing HADR is a tangible way to demonstrate Australia is a good neighbour (in the case of the Asia–Pacific region) and a good global citizen (in the case of the rest of the world). This willingness to help – underpinned by the cultural traditions of mateship and giving others a 'fair go' – is deeply embedded in the Australian psyche. While the focus of this book is Australian air power in HADR, air power is simply the capability: the means by which Australia often engages in HADR. This book is, in fact, about people: about those who are affected by disasters worldwide, about the Australian men and women who provide HADR and, essentially, about what it means to be human and to act humanely. For this reason, this book focuses on the qualitative over the quantitative: on how Australian air power helps people, rather than the technical details of aircraft or the number of HADR missions flown. (However, the appendices include lists of the military operations and aircraft included in this book, for those readers who love dates and numbers.) Many Australian men and women are proud of their personal involvement in HADR missions and, in fact, many are drawn to a career in the ADF with the specific hope they may be able to contribute to Australia's future HADR efforts. Members of the reserves are among those ADF personnel who make significant contributions to HADR operations by providing specialist skills that may not be readily available in the permanent forces, or which cannot be suddenly diverted from other tasking.[9] The ADF acknowledges one of the key reasons why it is able to so successfully undertake HADR missions is due to the individual quality of its personnel.[10] Reflecting on Operation *Sumatra Assist I*, following the devastating tsunami in the Indian Ocean on Boxing Day 2004, the former vice chief of the ADF, Vice Admiral Shalders, noted:

> I was once again struck by the human touch that our men and women bring to these sorts of operations. Their empathy, their compassion and their understanding for the plight of others were very evident.[11]

But in addition to altruistic motives, the Australian Government is aware it is in its own strategic interests to provide HADR to other countries: to promote both regional and global security and prosperity:

> [Australia's] decisions to undertake HA/DR missions and their nature, level and duration often not only reflect altruistic imperatives … but also their use as 'soft power' enablers in support of Australia's national interests.[12]

Because the Asia–Pacific region experiences more disasters than any other region in the world, Australia has frequent opportunities to engage in HADR, and thereby both demonstrate its altruism and promote regional security.[13] The *Stabilisation and Humanitarian Operations* doctrine confirms: 'Australia's security and prosperity is linked to the stability and security of the Indo-Pacific region.'[14]

The growing impact of climate change means the frequency of disasters will likely only increase in the future, and their scale magnify.[15] For the many island and archipelago nations throughout the Asia–Pacific region, rising sea levels, coastal erosion and increasing severe weather incidents (such as cyclones) are of particular concern. Basic human needs within the region must therefore continue to be met (food, clean water, medical aid, disease prevention, safe accommodation, and so on), all of which can be provided through HADR. To deny people these basic needs would not only be a violation of human rights but would also increase the likelihood of the impact of the disaster spreading to Australian territory. Australia is historically a preferred destination within the region for refugees fleeing disasters and crises in their own nations.[16] Australia is therefore likely to continue to engage in HADR, especially in the Asia–Pacific region, at an equivalent or greater level than it has in the past. As mentioned earlier, due to its unique transportation and logistical capabilities, the ADF is most frequently tasked to provide Australia's HADR efforts. But in certain circumstances, the Australian Government may also task commercial airlines to provide HADR.

Australian air power in different types of humanitarian aid and disaster relief

HADR is largely associated in people's minds with the provision of relief supplies, such as food, water and medical supplies and, indeed, this activity makes up a large proportion of Australia's HADR efforts. Air power is especially useful in the delivery of relief supplies because of its speed: aircraft can travel from Australia to a foreign country in hours whereas a ship may take days or even weeks. Even when shorter distances are involved, such as when the disaster occurs within Australian territory, aircraft (especially helicopters) can reach remote or inaccessible areas that may not be easily accessible via land or water. Larger helicopters, such as the Chinook, are especially valuable in certain HADR missions because of their significant lift capabilities.[17] The doctrine manual *ADF Air Power* states that air power is often 'the initial face of the ADF in a humanitarian assistance and disaster relief (HADR) operation, bringing the initial life-saving stores to an affected nation.'[18] In cases where aircraft cannot safely land to offload relief supplies, it is sometimes possible to deliver them via airdrop (dropping supplies out the back of an aircraft while it is in flight, where they parachute down to the ground). For these reasons, aircraft are:

> often the transportation mode of choice when speed, reach, and obstacle and surface threat avoidance are required. The air power attributes that are especially relevant to HA/DR missions include the ability to rapidly deploy, sustain and redeploy personnel and materiel [supplies] to, from or within an operational theatre.[19]

While the capabilities described here are largely the purview of the RAAF, the other ADF services also contribute meaningfully to airborne HADR missions, as do Australian commercial airlines (most notably Qantas). The non-aircraft assets which are especially valuable in supporting these missions are the RAN's ships, which can transport their own and the Army's helicopters, along with a significantly greater volume of relief supplies than can be loaded onto even the largest RAAF cargo aircraft, the C-17 Globemaster. As Australia's Sea Power Centre noted, 'although ships move at only one-thirtieth the speed of aircraft, they can carry thousands of times the payload.'[20] The RAN's ships have the added advantage of being able to fully sustain their crew for weeks or even months at a time, thereby avoiding adding to the logistical burden in the disaster location where the infrastructure and food and water supplies may have been significantly damaged or destroyed.[21] By contrast, if aircrew are required to stay at a disaster location for longer than the time it takes to deliver their cargo of relief supplies (for example, to enable them sufficient time to rest before flying home, in line with ADF safety policies), they must be accommodated (and often fed) using the available local resources, which may already be stretched to serve the affected local population.

Australian air power has been used to deliver relief supplies for decades, with early missions after the Second World War including Qantas's delivery of food parcels to Great Britain during its inaugural Sydney-to-London flight in 1947, and the *Berlin Airlift* of 1948–49 (during an attempt by the Soviet Union to starve civilians in Berlin to coerce them into switching allegiance). This book will also explore times when Australian aircraft airdropped relief supplies to populations in need, including during Operation *Okra* (after Yazidi refugees fled to barren Mount Sinjar in Iraq in 2014 to escape genocide by the Islamic State of Iraq and the Levant (ISIS)).

In addition to delivering relief supplies, air power can be used to evacuate at-risk or injured people, conduct aerial search-and-rescue missions, or repatriate the bodies of people killed during a disaster. Both the ADF and Qantas have historically been involved in evacuation missions. Due to its extensive international coverage, Qantas aircraft are often already on location in, or close to, affected areas at the time of a disaster and, as such, can start evacuating people while the ADF is still en route. Australian airborne-evacuation missions have included Australia's largest-ever peacetime evacuation (following Cyclone *Tracy* in Darwin in 1974) and Operation *Ramp* (during the Lebanon War in 2006). While Qantas has been involved in aeromedical evacuations in the past, today it is usually the RAAF – with its purpose-designed aircraft, including hospital-grade facilities and medical personnel – that provides this capability. Australian aeromedical-evacuation missions have included Operation *Babylift* (when Australia joined allied nations in evacuating Vietnamese orphans of war in 1975) and Operation *Bali Assist* (following the 2002 Bali bombings).

It is also usually the ADF that engages in aerial search-and-rescue and damage-assessment missions. The RAAF has specialised aircraft (such as the E-7A Wedgetail with its intelligence, surveillance and reconnaissance capabilities) which add value to these types of missions. But the RAN plays a significant role in supporting air power in ocean-based search-and-rescue missions due to its capability to transport helicopters (which can then engage in short sorties from the ship's deck) far from land and the nearest airbase or airfield. Aerial search-and-rescue missions featured in this book include the search for survivors during the 1996–97 Vendée Globe yacht race (when two competitors went missing separately in the deep Southern Ocean) and Operation *Southern Indian Ocean* (following the disappearance of Malaysia Airlines Flight 370 in 2014). Air Commodore Tony McCormack will also provide the conclusion to the prologue: the mission to rescue the German aviator in the South Pacific Ocean in 1997.

In the past, the Australian Government has tasked both commercial airlines and the ADF to repatriate the bodies of Australians who have lost their lives in disasters overseas. In this book are accounts of the use of Australian air power in repatriating Australian citizens through missions including Operation *Kokoda Assist* (following the crash of Airlines PNG Flight 4684 in 2009) and Operation *Bring Them Home* (following the crash of Malaysia Airlines Flight 17 in Ukraine in 2014).

Finally, the use of air power in HADR missions can also involve transporting personnel who have specific skillsets to the sites of disasters, for reasons as varied as providing medical aid, searching for survivors, or repairing damaged infrastructure. The ADF's engineers are especially valuable in the latter for their ability to generate clean drinking water and make damaged buildings and other infrastructure safe again. An additional advantage is that, as trained Defence personnel, they 'are capable of operating under the most demanding conditions.'[22] But, in many cases, the personnel who are transported to disaster locations are not military personnel, but rather civilians with specific skillsets. For example, civilian forensic investigators may be transported to a disaster location to investigate the circumstances that led to the disaster, to help prevent similar events in the future; this is particularly common following an aircraft crash. Medical personnel were transported via air during Operation *Sumatra Assist I* (following the Boxing Day tsunami in 2004) and Operation *Longreach* (following an earthquake in Pakistan in 2005). Search-and-rescue personnel were transported via air during Operation *Ashika Assist* (after the ferry *Princess Ashika* sank in Tonga in 2009) and Operation *Christchurch Assist* (following an earthquake in New Zealand in 2011). While not by definition *person*nel, search-and-rescue dogs may also be transported via air to assist in HADR missions, including the two who became 'the most famous dogs in Japan at the time' during Operation *Pacific Assist 2011* (after the meltdown of the Fukushima Daiichi Nuclear Power Plant).[23] Another key group who can add significant value to HADR missions are disaster-mitigation personnel, whose time-critical efforts may prevent the disaster from escalating into an even greater humanitarian crisis. These personnel have in the past included civilian firefighters during Operation *Bushfire Assist* (in Australia in early 2020) and ADF personnel during the COVID-19 pandemic, some of whom deployed to Christmas Island to help quarantine Australians who had evacuated from Wuhan in China.

PART I
WHY NATIONS ENGAGE IN HUMANITARIAN AID AND DISASTER RELIEF

Humanitarian aid and disaster relief throughout history

Since antiquity, nations have engaged in HADR as a strategy to achieve political outcomes, and especially to further their own national agendas.[1] From at least the time of Alexander the Great (356–28 CE), victorious armies have provided assistance to the people whom they have conquered, both soldiers and civilians, in an attempt to soften the blow of defeat and to earn their future cooperation.[2] This practice has continued into modern times. When the United States of America engaged in HADR in Europe during the First World War (1914–18), it aimed to demonstrate its military prowess as much as it aimed to extend its compassion to those in need.[3] After all, a nation that can afford to give away food and other precious supplies while engaged in a war far from home communicates to its enemies that it is well resourced for a long and taxing campaign. Similarly, during the interwar period (1918–39), when the United States engaged in HADR in countries which had formerly been their enemies, it aimed to earn the gratitude of the governments and civilians of those countries, in a bid for future peace.[4] For example, when the United States came to the aid of Romania immediately following the First World War, as well as bringing much-needed relief to civilians, it aimed to counter Bolshevism in the region by showing it – a democratic nation – still had plenty to share even after a prolonged and brutal war.[5] When the Australian Government tasked the ADF to provide HADR throughout South-East Asia between the mid-1950s and mid-1970s, its aim was similarly to both bolster the defences of allied nations in the region, and ease the suffering of citizens following decades of warfare.[6] Australia aimed to prevent the further spread of communism throughout the region by *directly* easing suffering and by *indirectly* demonstrating the advantages of democracy. While Australia's specific political motivations for engaging in HADR in the Asia–Pacific region may have changed, the mid-20th century represents the beginning of Australia's regular provision of HADR to its neighbours.

In addition to political motivations, for at least hundreds of years nations have also engaged in HADR for philosophical and religious reasons. By providing famine relief to Confucian households in parts of China in the late 16th century, local authorities hoped to ensure Confucianism would survive into the following generation.[7] In this way, the authorities were attempting to keep the Confucian system alive literally by keeping its adherents alive. Great Britain went a step further when it conducted HADR throughout its empire from the mid-19th century, by seeking not only to preserve a belief system, but also to add to its numbers.[8] That is, as well as seeking to fulfil its perceived duty of care for the various indigenous populations it had added to its empire, Great Britain also aimed to convert them to the state religion of Christianity.[9]

But nations have engaged in HADR throughout history for more than either political or philosophical reasons. For much of human history, the lives of many humans – especially females and people from certain ethnic and socio-economic backgrounds – were regarded by the more powerful members of society as having little or even no value. But with the rise of the Age of Enlightenment in the 17th century, people from all parts of European society started to understand and value the concept of 'humanity': of valuing human lives for their own sake.[10] From the 1650s, the more progressive-thinking European nations increasingly engaged in HADR as they came to acknowledge helping people in need is simply the right thing to do, separate to furthering a political agenda or winning converts.[11] Closely linked to the spread of the concept of humanity was the acceptance that humans – all humans everywhere, regardless of their race or religion or culture – have certain basic rights: 'human' rights.[12] With this increasing acceptance of universal human rights later arose socio-political movements such as the abolition of the African slave trade and the international suffrage movement.[13]

By the time Napoléon Bonaparte (1769–1821) had conquered much of Europe, HADR had evolved into a form which we would easily recognise today: to distribute relief supplies, often via military resources, to those who needed them.[14] Following the First World War, the need for humanitarian aid was so widespread, especially throughout war-torn Europe, that the global community demanded a new HADR strategy to meet the needs of as many of the millions of starving and displaced people as possible.[15] Foreign militaries and international humanitarian organisations increasingly demanded individual nations take ownership of any HADR efforts within their borders.[16] That is, while agencies who provided HADR willingly delivered relief supplies to nations in need, they increasingly expected those nations to ultimately take responsibility for easing the suffering of their own populations, by prioritising relief for those who had the most urgent need. This shifting of responsibility to individual governments established a pattern for HADR which continues around the world to this day.

Why nations engage in humanitarian aid and disaster relief today

As throughout history, many nations today engage in HADR for both altruistic and political reasons.[17] Only rarely today do nations engage in HADR for philosophical or religious reasons, although this may be a contributing motivator for private or faith-based humanitarian organisations and charities.

Today, most nations that engage in HADR do so predominantly to help others. The governments of these nations believe they have a moral obligation – as humans, as public servants, as members of the international community – to help others who are in need. Australia's Department of Foreign Affairs and Trade, for example, states Australia's humanitarian strategy seeks to save lives, to ease suffering and uphold human dignity during and following disasters and other humanitarian crises.[18] Other democratic nations have similar HADR strategies: the Department of Defense states the United States engages in HADR to uphold universality, impartiality and human dignity.[19]

But as well as altruistic reasons, many nations provide HADR as a strategy to safeguard or promote their own national and political interests. Disasters can pause, or even reverse, a nation's economic growth, and can contribute to serious and prolonged social and political instability within a region.[20] In a speech to the Parliament of Australia in 1950, former minister for external affairs, Sir Percy Spender, stated: '[Australia's] first and constant interest must be the security of our own homeland and the maintenance of peace in the area in which our country is geographically placed.'[21] One of the ways in which Australia still works towards the *security* and *peace* which Sir Percy identified is through HADR. Here is how it works. When Australia engages in HADR within the Asia–Pacific region, it strives to minimise the impact of the disaster which has just occurred, and to help the affected nation to prepare itself for future crises.[22] Australia's HADR efforts also allow Australians to express solidarity, and build positive working relationships, with other nations and their governments, their militaries and their civilians.[23] Further, by engaging in HADR within the Asia–Pacific region, Australia indirectly works to safeguard its borders from a potential influx of refugees fleeing from any ongoing effects of the disaster.[24] The reasoning is if a population's human needs are being met within the borders of their own country, they will be less motivated to seek refuge in a different country. Through these means, Australia thereby uses HADR to promote stability and future prosperity within the region.[25] By extension, Australia indirectly uses HADR as part of its defence strategy: to promote security and peace without using traditional offensive or 'military' tactics.[26]

Similarly to Australia, the United States asserts it uses HADR to promote security on a regional and even a global scale.[27] The United Kingdom takes a slightly different approach, stating it uses HADR to prevent bad situations from potentially becoming even worse.[28] But their intended outcomes are the same. These nations, along with many other nations who engage in HADR as a political strategy, recognise disasters can lead to poverty and social and political instability.[29] This poverty and instability may prompt a struggling and discontented population to pursue violence, which can lead to widespread and even worldwide outcomes, such as global terrorism and war.[30] One notable example is that of the international movement attributed to Islamic State of Iraq and the Levant (better known as Islamic State or ISIS). Thousands of men and women from throughout the Middle East joined ISIS in an effort to counter the poverty and displacement they experienced during and following the Iraq War (2003–11), the Arab Spring (2010–12) and the Syrian Civil War (2011–) by using the political strategy of terrorism. As ISIS grew in strength, lethality and notoriety, its members and affiliates conducted significant terrorist attacks far beyond the Middle East region, such as the coordinated attacks in France which killed 130 people in Paris in 2015 and 86 people in Nice in 2016. Yet the provision of responsive and proportionate HADR following a disaster may prevent subsequent political crises such as terrorism or war.[31] HADR can achieve this by both meeting the immediate physical needs of a population (such as food and medical care) and by supporting a nation's longer-term prosperity by rebuilding critical infrastructure and establishing stores of emergency supplies to safeguard against future disasters.[32]

A third reason why nations today may choose to engage in HADR is to be seen by the rest of the world to be doing a good and caring thing. The United Kingdom's Ministry of Defence stated in a recent report that, 'there may be specific UK interest in contributing, and being seen to contribute, to a disaster response.'[33] And in fact, nations generally consider other nations which consistently and generously engage in HADR to hold high standing within the international community.[34]

Regardless of why nations choose to engage in HADR – whether for altruistic, political or other reasons – the United Nations Office for the Coordination of Humanitarian Affairs (OCHA) states all who engage in HADR should adhere to certain strict humanitarian principles.[35] It asserts that following these principles is necessary to ensure the outcomes are human lives saved and human sufferings eased.[36]

OCHA proposes the following four principles:

1. Humanity: Human suffering must be addressed wherever it is found. The purpose of humanitarian action is to protect life and health and ensure respect for human beings.
2. Neutrality: Humanitarian actors must not take sides in hostilities or engage in controversies of a political, racial, religious or ideological nature.
3. Impartiality: Humanitarian action must be carried out on the basis of need alone, giving priority to the most urgent cases of distress and making no distinctions on the basis of nationality, race, gender, religious belief, class or political opinions.
4. Operational independence: Humanitarian action must be autonomous from the political, economic, military or other objectives that any actor may hold with regard to areas where humanitarian action is being implemented.[37]

The link between the military and humanitarian aid and disaster relief

As seen earlier, militaries have engaged in HADR since at least the time of Alexander the Great in the 4th century, and their efforts had become well organised and highly efficient by the time of Napoléon Bonaparte in the 18th century.[38] Long before the end of the First World War, there arose an immense need for HADR, especially throughout Europe, as nations struggled to feed both their soldiers at the front and their civilians back home. Following the end of the war in 1918, millions of men – the traditional primary income earners for most families – returned to their homes physically or mentally injured. Many never returned home at all. This led to millions of families struggling to earn sufficient money to survive, and many nations lacking the necessary manpower to rebuild the vital infrastructure which had been damaged or destroyed.[39] To meet the many and complex needs of this post-war world, HADR necessarily became increasingly professionalised and internationalised.[40] It became highly organised on a global scale. It was therefore a natural fit for militaries, with their extensive logistical and transportation resources, and their traditionally organised and hands-on methodology, to become increasingly involved in delivering HADR.[41]

During the 20th century – a century characterised by many wars and humanitarian crises – so frequently were foreign militaries involved in HADR that, by the end of the Cold War in 1991, the international community had widely come to *expect* militaries would engage in international HADR as one of their key functions.[42] This is also the case on an intra-national level. For many nations today, including France, the United States and many countries in the Asia–Pacific region, their individual militaries serve a central role in their domestic HADR efforts.[43] But for some nations, including many Asian nations, the military is their *only* domestic provider of organised HADR.[44] Yet when these nations experience large-scale disasters, their military may not be able to cope singlehandedly with its many humanitarian needs, and they may therefore call for (or accept offers of) assistance from those foreign governments with whom they have a trusted relationship.[45] The default response for many of these foreign governments, such as Australia, is to send their own militaries to help. But OCHA, the United Kingdom's Ministry of Defence and the North Atlantic Treaty Organization (NATO) all agree a nation which has experienced a disaster should request the assistance of foreign militaries only when no comparable civilian alternatives are available.[46] Yet at the same time, the Ministry of Defence acknowledges militaries possess unique professional, organisational and logistical skills that add value to HADR efforts.[47] NATO, however, asserts just because a foreign military has the *capability* to engage in HADR does not mean it has the *right*.[48] NATO's caution originates from its concern that foreign militaries, who exist to serve their corresponding governments, may be either unable or unwilling, or both, to adhere to OCHA's four humanitarian principles as outlined in the previous section: especially the principle of operational independence.[49] As a reminder, this principle explicitly states: 'Humanitarian action must be autonomous from the political, economic, military or other objectives that any actor may hold with regard to areas where humanitarian action is being implemented.'[50] In other words, the goal of HADR must be to save lives and to relieve suffering, not to further the agendas of foreign militaries or their governments. The authors of the academic article 'Military Provision of Humanitarian Assistance and Disaster Relief in Non-Conflict Crises' asserted:

> Opposition to military participation in humanitarian endeavors is due to the fact that the use of military assistance within that context has a dark side. Namely, it suggests the use of politically influenced force behind such interventions.[51]

But despite this potential conflict of interest, the default response for many – even most – nations who engage in HADR is to send their militaries. Many nations would argue their military simply has the best capabilities to provide international HADR and they have no ulterior motives, political or otherwise.

PART II

AUSTRALIAN AIR POWER IN HUMANITARIAN AID AND DISASTER RELIEF SINCE THE SECOND WORLD WAR

Chapter 1

DELIVERY AND AIRDROP OF RELIEF SUPPLIES

After a nation has experienced a disaster, its population frequently needs relief supplies – food, clean water, medical supplies, tents and so on – as soon as they can be delivered.[1] For this reason, Australia most frequently transports relief supplies via air. After all, aircraft can travel to any location within Australia, or from Australia to a foreign country, within hours. A ship may take days or even weeks. And aircraft (especially helicopters) can reach remote areas which may not be accessible by road, rail or sea.

I. The Australian Defence Force delivering relief supplies

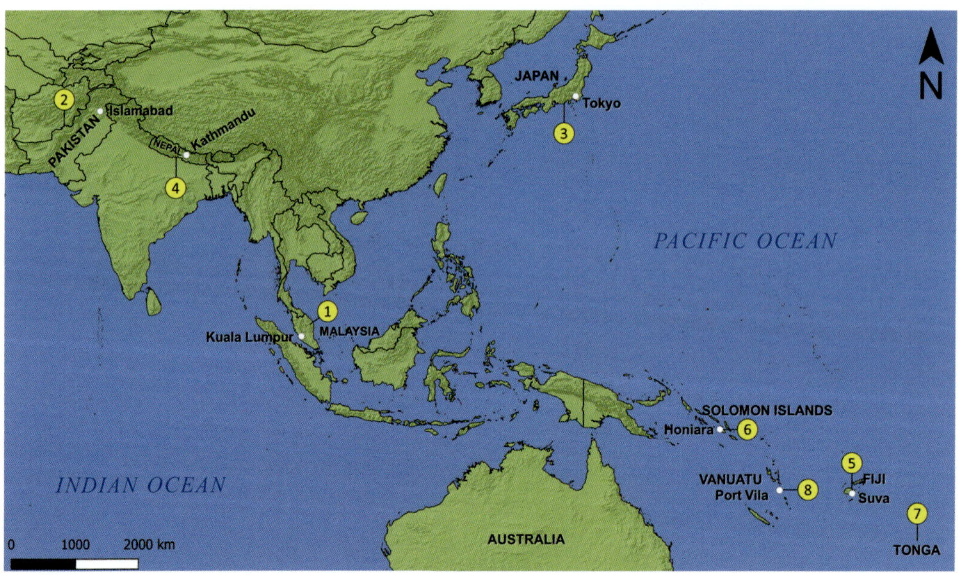

Selected Australian Defence Force missions to deliver relief supplies: Asia–Pacific

1. Operation *Bad Water*, Malaysia, 1967
2. Operation *Pakistan Assist I*, 2005–6 & Operation *Bushranger*, 2006
3. Operation *Pacific Assist 2011*, Japan
4. Operation *Nepal Assist*, 2015
5. Operation *Fiji Assist 2016* & Operation *Fiji Assist 2020*
6. Operation *Lilia*, Solomon Islands, 2021–22
7. Operation *Tonga Assist 2022*
8. Operation *Vanuatu Assist 2023*

By virtue of its extensive air-power capabilities and its mandate to serve the Australian Government, the Australian Defence Force (ADF) is the Australian entity which has traditionally played the largest role in delivering relief supplies via air.

To our neighbours

In part because many nations in the Asia–Pacific region have limited financial and logistical resources to enable them to cope in the aftermath of a disaster, and in part because it is in the same geographical region, when Australia delivers relief supplies it most frequently delivers them to neighbouring countries.[2]

Since the earliest days of using air power for humanitarian aid and disaster relief (HADR) missions, these deliveries have often included essential medical supplies. After Mount Lamington erupted in New Guinea in 1951, 3,000 people in the territories of Papua and New Guinea lost their lives due to injuries sustained from the eruption and illnesses from water and crops contaminated by volcanic ash. Medical supplies were urgently needed to prevent further deaths from the eruption and subsequent ash poisoning. In response, the Royal Australian Air Force (RAAF) used two Douglas C-47 Dakotas to deliver much-needed blood plasma donated by the Australian Red Cross.[3] In a similar incident, floods in Malaysia in 1967 killed 38 people and displaced 320,000 more, with contaminated water making many more thousands of people sick. In the HADR mission Operation *Bad Water*, the RAAF delivered 40,000 doses of the typhoid vaccine via Lockheed C-130 Hercules to help prevent further illnesses and deaths throughout the country.[4] In the 21st century, the ADF stood up an international HADR effort, Operation *COVID-19 Assist* (2020–22), in response to the global pandemic. This operation took many forms which will be explored throughout this book, but one crucial aspect was distributing the COVID-19 vaccine. In just one example in the Asia–Pacific region, the RAAF delivered 10,000 doses of the vaccine to Samoa via an Airbus KC-30A Multi-Role Tanker Transport in 2021.[5] These vaccines were distributed throughout Samoa as part of its vaccination program.[6]

When Australia embarks on HADR missions, it is often just one of many other nations providing assistance in the same place at the same time; this is most often the case following large-scale disasters. The 2004 Boxing Day tsunami in the Indian Ocean was the most devastating in recent history, killing up to 230,000 people.[7] During Operation *Sumatra Assist I*, within just 36 hours of the tsunami making landfall, the RAAF delivered essential relief supplies to Indonesia via four C-130H Hercules aircraft.[8] Australia was just one nation in a global coalition involved in this HADR effort, with support coming from as far away as Europe.

More recently, following the eruption of the Hunga Tonga–Hunga Ha'apai underwater volcano in January 2022, Australia worked with the militaries of New Caledonia and Fiji to provide aid to Tonga. Through Operation *Tonga Assist 2022*, the ADF, the French Armed Forces in New Caledonia and the Republic of Fiji Military Forces operated together from the Royal Australian Navy's (RAN) HMAS *Canberra* – while RAAF aircrew

Flying Officer Jorge Elosegui Guerra

Royal Australian Air Force

Flying Officer Jorge Elosegui Guerra (Defence)

We are here to serve. We are far away from many other parts of the world which are much more populated than us, and we need to ensure that we look after each other. Australians are famous for being generous and friendly, and responses such as this align with our 'mateship' attitude.[12]

Mission: Operation *Tonga Assist 2022*

Flying Officer Elosegui Guerra was the officer in charge of the air movements section at RAAF Amberley in Queensland during Operation Tonga Assist 2022*, the ADF's HADR mission following a volcanic eruption and tsunami in the island nation.*

I was having lunch at the mess [dining room] with the other flying officer in my air movements section – we were both new as it was our first week in our roles – when our boss, the flight commander, called us and asked us to rush back to our office to prepare a team to deploy to Tonga. It was January 2022 and many of the section's members were still trying to understand the dynamics of the squadron, which posed an extra challenge. I had to quickly learn all of our interactions with the different stakeholders, such as the Department of Foreign Affairs and Trade (DFAT), who are in charge of arranging humanitarian-response stores, and other departments in the Air Force which have to come together to get an aircraft up in the air for this type of mission.

Members who deployed had around 24 hours' notice, and we had the first aircraft scheduled to depart that weekend, although the first flights were delayed due to volcanic ash in the air and on the runway in Tonga.

We received the cargo from the DFAT contractor, then when we had the cargo in the terminal, we built it on aircraft pallets to be rolled into the aircraft itself. Once we got confirmation of what type of aircraft was going on the mission, my team did the load planning to ensure the cargo met the weight and balance specifications for the aircraft. Whenever possible, we did this the night before, to allow for an early departure and a return on the same day.

The first aircraft were C-130 Hercules from RAAF Base Richmond in New South Wales, and once the ash in the air and on the runway in Tonga improved, we started using C-17 Globemasters. For each of the missions, my air movements section deployed at least five members. The cargo included a forklift, manual earthmoving equipment (shovels and wheelbarrows), FOD*BOSSes (tools to swipe runways and taxiways) to clean ash at the airport, a lot of bottled water, long-life food rations, blankets and clothing.

The entire HADR mission took roughly one month, and my section was involved for the duration. We – and the whole of the RAAF – were praised for the quick response and the hard work we put into this mission.

One challenge was that COVID-19 restrictions in Tonga were very strict due to a low percentage of the population being vaccinated at that point in time, which meant some of the flights were delayed or cancelled due to crewmembers being close contacts to people who had tested positive to the virus.

Something that made the whole mission unusual is the foreign forces who used RAAF Amberley as their forward operating base. Japan brought two C-130 Hercules aircraft to do taps in and out of Tonga from the base. They were supported by bigger Japanese military aircraft which kept bringing supplies. My team had to work to shuffle cargo among these aircraft.

My role as the officer in charge included acting as the point of contact for the Japanese contingent and ensuring all parties had clear information of what they could do on any given mission. For my team members deploying to Tonga, I had to ensure work and rest rations were abided by, and that we were still meeting our capability on base.

During the mission, we proved Australia looks after its neighbours in the Pacific when they are in need. We also strengthened bonds with our Asian neighbours and showed we can collaborate to help countries in the region. Engaging in HADR is the right thing to do as we are the biggest country in the region. Also, part of the Australian population originated from neighbouring countries; these citizens and residents are taxpayers too, and Australia has an obligation to them to ensure their home countries are provided with assistance when needed.

Ultimately, HADR has a big strategic impact in accordance with the Australian Government's aim to shape a climate of peace and collaboration within the region. We are here to serve. We are far away from many other parts of the world which are much more populated than us, and we need to ensure we look after each other. Australians are famous for being generous and friendly, and responses such as this align with our 'mateship' attitude.[13]

flew separate sorties – to deliver more than 370 tonnes of relief supplies.[9] Other nations from the Asia–Pacific region, including Japan, also provided assistance.[10] The Australian High Commissioner to Tonga, Rachael Moore, stated during the HADR mission:

> We help each other out in the Pacific. Australia is proud to work alongside our Pacific family to contribute to the Government of Tonga's timely and effective response.[11]

RAAF personnel unloading a C-130H Hercules at Banda Aceh International Airport in Indonesia during Operation *Sumatra Assist I* in 2004 (Defence)

Also in 2022, Australia joined the United Kingdom, United States, Canada and many European nations in providing HADR to Ukraine following the invasion by Russia in February of that year. After receiving a request for help from the Government of Ukraine, RAAF aircraft delivered military supplies – including missiles and other weapons and 20 Bushmaster protected mobility vehicles – as well as medical supplies, tents, food and water. Before the Bushmasters were loaded onto the RAAF aircraft, their original Australian camouflage pattern was repainted olive, and a Ukrainian flag and the words 'United with Ukraine' in both English and Ukrainian were added.[14]

Constant training and maintaining operational readiness have equipped the ADF to be able to deploy on HADR missions at short notice, as in Operation *Sumatra Assist I* following the Boxing Day tsunami in the Indian Ocean. This was also the case during Operation *Pacific Assist 2011*. In March 2011, a magnitude-9.0 earthquake struck off the north-east coast of Tōhoku in Japan and triggered a 12-storey-tall tsunami and the subsequent meltdown of the Fukushima Daiichi Nuclear Power Plant. In response to this multifaceted disaster, which killed 20,000 people, the RAAF rapidly deployed a fleet of Boeing C-17A Globemaster IIIs with 450 tonnes of relief supplies.[15] The officer in charge of Operation *Pacific Assist 2011*, Wing Commander David Howard, stated: 'The C-17 enabled us to move significant amounts of cargo … to the places they need[ed] to be to help the Japanese people as quickly as possible.'[16]

Air Commodore Tony McCormack

Royal Australian Air Force

Colonel Hiroyoshi Ohura from the Japan Air Self-Defense Force (right) thanking Tony McCormack (then a group captain, left) for the RAAF's assistance during Operation *Pacific Assist 2011* (Defence)

The Empress of Japan spotted the 'Australia' flash on my uniform, stopped in front of me, bowed and thanked me for all that I and Australia had done for Japan.[17]

Mission: Operation *Pacific Assist 2011*

After an earthquake and subsequent tsunami triggered the meltdown of the Fukushima Daiichi Nuclear Power Plant, Air Commodore Tony McCormack, then a group captain based in Japan, participated heavily in Australia's HADR mission.

The earthquake on 11 March 2011 that led to Operation *Pacific Assist 2011* was violent. I was watching the glass in windows flexing, trees vibrating and power lines flexing from loose to taut. The entire building was moving and I and all of my staff took shelter. When the initial shaking stopped, we left the building, waited for a bit to make sure there were no aftershocks, and then went back to our office. We turned the TV on to see where the epicentre was and whether there had been any damage – only to watch the live coverage of the tsunami. It was then we realised this was an enormous disaster and there would be a relief effort.

Less than an hour after the earthquake had struck, Australia's Defence Attaché to Japan called me and asked if I and my family were safe and whether there was any damage at the Yokota Air Base, where I was stationed. He said Australia was planning to send one or two C-17 Globemasters to Yokota within the next 24 to 48 hours.

In my official role as Commander of United Nations Command Rear, my job was to support and manage the flow of United Nations military forces to and from Korea in the event of renewed conflict on the Korean Peninsula. Providing assistance to Japan in the event of a humanitarian disaster was outside the scope of my role. However, I had a choice: I could sit back and say it was not my responsibility, or I could assist (and sitting back when someone needs help is not what Australians do). Due to the earthquake, I had lost contact with my boss in Korea to be able to seek his guidance and approval, so I unilaterally decided I and my team would assist in the relief effort. The evening of 11 March was eerily quiet as plans were being made; it wasn't until early the following morning that requests for our support started arriving.

Australia provided three C-17s: one delivered an urban search-and-rescue (USAR) team and then flew HADR sorties in Japan, and two delivered a high-pressure water pump to help cool the reactors at the nuclear power plant. Also on board the C-17s were two search-and-rescue dogs, RAAF aircrew, ground crew, an air load team, operations officers, a medical officer, and others to support the aircraft.

To get the RAAF C-17s into Yokota at short notice was incredibly complex. We needed to arrange transit accommodation for the USAR team; base access for civilians; customs, immigration and quarantine, including quarantine for the dogs; kennels for the dogs; support for the USAR team and RAAF personnel; and myriad other things. We approached this methodically and worked through each issue to make sure it would happen.

Initially, my role was to get the Australian and New Zealand USAR teams into the country and then to the disaster area. Another task was looking after the C-17s and RAAF personnel so they could accomplish their mission. Additionally, I was the liaison between about eight countries and the United States Forces Japan to coordinate support and assistance. I was also communicating directly with Australia's Chief of Air Force and Chief of Defence Force when the circumstances required it. Finally, my team and I did whatever needed to be done to support the relief effort where and when we could. I spent some time in the disaster area, delivering aid from United States Marine Corps helicopters. Flying over the disaster area was a sobering experience: seeing the outline of hundreds of foundations of where houses once had been, fishing boats swept kilometres inland and large ships that had been lifted by the tsunami and placed hundreds of metres away from the wharf. When we landed to offload the relief supplies, Japanese civilians in their dozens appeared and efficiently offloaded the supplies we were carrying, allowing us to then quickly return for another load. I was impressed by their resilience in the face of the disaster.

I found the more we did, the more we found to do. It was hard, constant work, with multiple aftershocks and concerns about having another big earthquake and, of course, the situation [meltdown] at the power plant at Fukushima. Each day, I would write a summary of what my team was doing and what the countries we were liaising with were doing and planning. I discovered later that this daily email was receiving global distribution as I was one of a few who were coordinating efforts.

The Japanese military and civilians at Yokota Air Base thanked me often for what I was doing and for Australia's support. For months afterwards, I was thanked by Japanese people from across all areas of society for the support Australia had given in Japan's time of need. Once while I was attending a Japanese reception, the Empress of Japan spotted the 'Australia' flash on my uniform, stopped in front of me, bowed and thanked me for all that I and Australia had done for Japan.

Offshore HADR is a vital part of what the ADF does. Australia is one of the largest and most capable nations in the Indo–Pacific. When disaster strikes, other nations often lack the capacity and capability to respond. Australia can, and does, respond. Operation *Pacific Assist 2011* proved Australia is a reliable and responsible friend who will assist when and where we are needed. The worldwide response assisted Japan in the immediate aftermath of the triple disaster and this aid, support and comfort continue to this day.[18]

Frequently, as was the case during Operation *Tonga Assist 2022*, two or even all three of the ADF services – RAN, Army and RAAF – will deploy together on an HADR mission to deliver relief supplies. When Category 5 Severe Tropical Cyclone *Winston* struck the South Pacific in 2016, it was the southern hemisphere's strongest cyclone in recorded history.[19] It killed 44 people and displaced or otherwise affected more than 60% of the population of Fiji.[20] During Operation *Fiji Assist 2016*, in addition to the RAAF's C-17 Globemasters, the RAN used HMAS *Canberra* to transport more than 114 tonnes of relief supplies to Fiji which the Army then distributed via MRH-90 Taipan helicopters.[21] The helicopters were particularly valuable during this HADR mission in enabling the delivery of relief supplies to remote and difficult-to-access locations throughout the island nation.[22] A similar joint mission was Operation *Fiji Assist 2020*, following Category 5 Severe Tropical Cyclone *Yasa*, which killed four people in the South Pacific. During this operation, the Army delivered 78 tonnes of relief supplies via MRH-90 Taipans which it launched from the deck of HMAS *Adelaide*.[23] Army pilot Captain Matthew Dwyer observed: 'With the MRH-90s, we could reach more areas quickly, particularly those that were hard to reach by other means.'[24] Indeed, this tandem use of ship and helicopter is one of the most effective in delivering relief supplies in many situations, for both the size of the payload and the flexibility of its delivery.

An Australian Army MRH-90 Taipan launching from the flight deck of HMAS *Adelaide* to deliver relief supplies to the island of Vanua Levu in Fiji during Operation *Fiji Assist 2020* (Defence)

The ADF is well known for operating efficiently and effectively in these types of HADR missions. After Tropical Cyclones *Judy* and *Kevin* struck Vanuatu in the same week in early 2023, the ADF embarked on Operation *Vanuatu Assist 2023*. The RAAF immediately deployed cargo aircraft loaded with relief supplies to the capital city, Port Vila, while HMAS *Canberra* brought three Army CH-47 Chinook helicopters and additional supplies to deliver to remote areas with the greatest need.[25] Australia's defence minister, The Honourable Richard Marles, stated:

> The ADF personnel on board bring recent experience from other relief efforts in the region over the past two years. Defence is proud to support a member of the Pacific family.[26]

While some humanitarian crises may be predicted and planned for – even with only a few hours' notice – many more take the affected populations entirely by surprise. Natural disasters occur according to their own timetable. For this reason, and especially when the humanitarian crises are particularly serious, Australia will sometimes embark on more than one HADR mission at a time. When the RAAF delivered 13 pallets of relief supplies to Vanuatu following Category 5 Severe Tropical Cyclone *Harold* in 2020, which killed dozens of people across four nations, the ADF was concurrently supporting Operation *COVID-19 Assist* back home in Australia.[29]As Group Captain Anthony Bull stated during the mission: 'Despite these challenging times, it is rewarding to be able to deliver assistance to our Pacific neighbours.'[30] On rarer occasions, Australia will even be tasked to engage in more than one HADR operation in a single country at the same time. A recent example was during Operation *Lilia*, a joint mission by DFAT, the Australian Federal Police and the ADF in 2021 to support the Royal Solomon Islands Police Force to stabilise unrest in the capital city, Honiara. Following a COVID-19 outbreak in the island nation in early 2022, an additional 60 ADF personnel deployed to the Solomon Islands on RAAF Alenia C-27J Spartans to deliver more than 50 tonnes of food and emergency medical supplies.[31] Operation *Lilia*'s task force commander, Lieutenant Colonel Steve Frankel, acknowledged the ADF's capability to engage in multiple HADR missions simultaneously:

> The initial response to successfully help restore order after the November civil unrest shows that the ADF is able to rapidly respond to situations impacting the security of our Pacific family. Defence has broadened its focus to also assist the whole-of-Australian Government response to the growing COVID-19 outbreak here.[32]

Around the globe

While Australia has historically focused on delivering relief supplies throughout the Asia–Pacific region, it does not limit itself to only helping our neighbours: in exceptional circumstances, the Australian Government may task the ADF to deliver relief supplies beyond our part of the world. One of the earliest of such missions is also one of the most famous. The Berlin Blockade of 1948–49 was an attempt by the Soviet Union to starve civilians in the parts of Berlin in Germany which were under the control of the Western

Captain Jace Hutchison

Royal Australian Navy

The prime minister of Vanuatu, The Honourable Alatoi Ishmael Kalsakau Ma'aukora (left), presenting Commanding Officer HMAS *Canberra*, Captain Jace Hutchison (centre), and Commander Land Forces, Colonel Douglas Pashley (right), with gifts during a farewell ceremony following Operation *Vanuatu Assist 2023* (Defence)

I continue to be amazed by our personnel who generate goodwill towards Australia just by turning up with a friendly smile and a willingness to work to help people. You can see the effect this has on the ground, and it's good for our people too.[27]

Mission: Operation *Vanuatu Assist 2023*

Captain Jace Hutchison dual-commanded the relief effort Operation Vanuatu Assist 2023 *after Tropical Cyclones* Judy *and* Kevin *struck the island nation in rapid succession.*

Because HMAS *Canberra* is a primary HADR asset, we pay very close attention to significant weather patterns, particularly during the high-risk weather season. When Tropical Cyclones *Judy* and *Kevin* hit Vanuatu, we were not the assigned HADR response vessel, so while we were aware of the cyclone damage and the likelihood of an ADF response, the tip off by our higher headquarters (about 24 hours before we were officially activated) came as a surprise. Our official activation occurred on 2 March 2023 and we sailed with the full joint force, vehicles, equipment and HADR stores on 5 March.

The departure point of HMAS *Canberra* was Sydney, so the 5th Aviation Regiment (5AVN) with their three CH-47 Chinook helicopters deployed from Townsville in Queensland. The majority of maintenance equipment was transported by road and the aircraft flew separately to join us. As you can imagine, three aircraft with all of their personnel and maintenance equipment is a very large and cumbersome beast to move and establish in a new location – but absolutely necessary for the type of heavy-lift response we needed to provide.

In addition to personnel from HMAS *Canberra* and 5AVN, we also had on board personnel from the Headquarters Australian Amphibious Force (HQAAF), the 6th Engineer Support Regiment (6ESR), a small boat platoon, an underwater damage-repair element, an amphibious beach team, a deployable geospatial team, personnel from the Maritime Operational Health Unit, along with personnel from the ADF's cyber, intelligence, public affairs and imagery units. All up, we had a team of about 650 personnel on board. We also had remote support from the RAAF in the form of bulk HADR stores lift, reconnaissance and force sustainment.

In this particular case, I was the Commander Task Group (CTG) of the maritime elements, working in a dual-command role with the CTG of the land elements (primarily based on Army engineers from 6ESR and led by the Commander Landing Force (CLF) from HQAAF). Once we arrived in Vanuatu, the CLF moved his headquarters ashore to work closely with Australia's High Commission, the Australian Defence Attaché to Vanuatu and local government authorities, providing direction and guidance to my afloat headquarters so we could plan and execute our daily operations.

For most HADR missions, we generally aim for four to six weeks of deployment to provide immediate relief. This might mean two or three weeks on station [in location] providing that support, but you can never tell until you are in a position to make an informed assessment as the operation progresses and the host nation is reliably seen to be getting back on its own two feet. In consultation with the Department of Foreign Affairs and Trade (DFAT) and local authorities, non-government agencies and commercial companies will also provide support (such as intra-island ferries and air links). Expansion of their operations is generally a good sign that the conditions are being set for the transition to recovery, allowing for an ADF withdrawal of response forces. In this particular case, we were away for four weeks, with the Commander of Joint Operations keen to have all elements home by Easter.

The journey to Vanuatu took around four days, during which time we took the opportunity to plan and prepare the force for what was to come, with the return journey always used to clean and maintain equipment in preparation for clearing customs and quarantine in Australia and redeploying to our home units.

Life on board is good for embarked personnel. The ship is large and comfortable at sea, even in rough conditions. Water, when used correctly and not wasted, is plentiful. Personnel can achieve physical training regimes which can be followed up by laundry and bathing. Troops returning from the shore are prioritised to receive clean uniforms, hot meals, showers and beds. Chefs (drawn from the RAN and Army) cook four meals a day, providing high-quality food to the force.

As the commanding officer of the enabling platform, I am essentially responsible for the preparation, projection and sustainment of the force. In purely tactical terms, this means we manoeuvre the ship into locations from where we can conduct aviation, landing-craft and small-boat operations by day and night. We internally prepare and deliver HADR stores, equipment, food, vehicles and personnel into remote and outlying islands. We will also support the movement and hosting of dignitaries (such as the prime minister and DFAT personnel), local government authorities and civilian organisations.

Transporting helicopters via ship and then launching them from the deck is highly complex. When you put Army airframes into a maritime environment, in an enclosed space, with competing priorities and environmental restrictions, you must work extremely hard to carefully orchestrate the daily plan for maintenance, aircraft deck movements, stores and equipment loading, personnel loading and, of course, launching and recovering. CH-47 helicopters cannot be stowed below deck unless you remove the blades [rotors], so this creates its own set of problems with additional exposure in the maritime environment, and restricts personnel movement on deck.

These types of operations are inevitably aviation heavy: we rely on helicopters to be able to quickly lift significant amounts of equipment and personnel over vast distances and into remote and outlying islands. We are talking in some cases about hundreds of miles over water, through or around inclement tropical weather and into tricky landing zones that may or may not have been prepared appropriately. There is a high level of focus on operational risk management to ensure we can achieve this type of response safely while maintaining the momentum required to meet the mission's objectives (as well as DFAT's and the Australian Government's objectives).

Overall, this was a highly successful ADF deployment to support the DFAT-led mission to assist the Government of Vanuatu. We provided a meaningful response which had a profound effect on the local populace who were in great need of assistance – particularly those in remote areas who were completely cut off, who had suffered significant community or private infrastructure damage and who had lost their market gardens and were experiencing food scarcity.

The communities we visited were welcoming, friendly and grateful for our assistance. Every aspect of interaction by Australian military personnel with the local population and authorities was positive. This is a testament to the great character of our Australian servicemen and servicewomen, who are always adept at making friends and impressing with their professionalism wherever they go. I continue to be amazed by our personnel who generate goodwill towards Australia just by turning up with a friendly smile and a willingness to work to help people. You can see the effect this has on the ground, and it's good for our people too. And when you hear in the Prime Minister of Vanuatu's farewell speech that he is genuinely grateful for Australia's assistance, you really do feel you might have made a difference.

Professional militaries are the only organisations capable of responding quickly to these types of disasters in this type of remote maritime environment. They alone have the assets capable of conducting heavy lift of HADR stores, equipment, vehicles and personnel across large archipelagos spread over hundreds of miles of ocean. In the southwest Pacific, it will always fall to Australia to provide that large-scale, rapid response: there is no one else in this region with the capacity to achieve what the ADF can do.

We should be very proud of our Australian servicemen and servicewomen. When they are in these communities – such as our Army engineers on the ground in Port Vila and in Futuna and the other islands – they do a fantastic job, not just in their core roles but also as diplomats for Australia. They represent the Australian people amazingly well and I hear nothing but positive feedback from local communities and their government representatives.[28]

Wing Commander Stuart Wheal

Royal Australian Air Force

Lieutenant Colonel Steve Frankel (second from left) welcoming Wing Commander Stuart Wheal (centre) to Honiara International Airport in the Solomon Islands in 2022. They bump elbows, instead of shaking hands, in line with health guidance during the global COVID-19 pandemic (Defence)

Knowing that Aussies are there to support our neighbours in any way possible just makes me smile. And then hearing of the positive impact we had on the population of the Solomon Islands makes it even more special. We are always ready to help. I think it's the Aussie nature.[33]

Mission: COVID-19 support during Operation *Lilia*, 2022

Wing Commander Stuart Wheal served as the commanding officer during a mission to transport urgent medical supplies to the Solomon Islands following an outbreak of COVID-19 in the island nation. Australia was already engaged in the HADR mission Operation Lilia *– to help stabilise unrest – at the time.*

Our component of Operation *Lilia* involved getting much-needed COVID-19 supplies from Solomon Island's capital city, Honiara, to the other islands.

Our preparation to deploy was rather rapid and involved a very quick shift in focus. In the weeks leading up to the deployment, No 382 Squadron was the lead element for a possible Air Force contribution to Tonga following the eruption of the underwater volcano in January 2022. We had just taken a deep breath after being informed we would not be used for Operation *Tonga Assist 2022*, when we started hearing Australia may support the Solomon Islands following a COVID-19 outbreak. Our formal notice was only about four days, but the team was picking up on signals that made us start to prepare.

We had spent the year prior involved in exercises and preparing ourselves to be the Contingency Response Squadron, who would take the lead in any short-notice requirement. Swinging the preparation focus from a possible response in Tonga to another in the Solomon Islands was hectic yet rewarding. Watching the squadron members prepare was amazing; the majority of people knew what to do to make sure we were even more ready than we were before.

The planning cycle is evolutionary. We are always refining the plan as more information comes to hand. When we first heard of our potential activation, we had to look at what tasks were going to be given to us (without being told formally yet). This helped us to put together the team who would be required. We knew we would need security for the aircraft, and people to load them. As we would be away from home, communications were also a must. Then, questions were asked about how we would feed our team and fuel the aircraft; this led to the requirement for logistics experts. This continued as the logistics team looked at what equipment was needed for us to operate and how much aircraft space was going to be allocated. It was positive to know the ADF already had troops on the ground in Honiara (the main focus of Operation *Lilia* was to help stabilise civil unrest), which meant there were some vital items, such as a forklift, already there.

On the day we left, I was on the phone to the commander of the Air Operations Centre, formally being given my command responsibility of the Air Component. I went from being the commander of the airbase operations component, to the commander of the entire Air Force contribution. That meant I had two C-27 Spartans from No 35 Squadron, and the 20 people they came with, as part of my direct team. The people are always the best memory of any deployment and this one was no different. The aircraft maintainers worked hard to ensure the two C-27s were ready each day: for the two weeks of operations, there was only one day when one of the aircraft was unserviceable. The remaining 30 people were from the combat support element and included security, an air load team, medical, logistics, personnel support, communications, operations and some airfield surveyors (as we would go to remote islands where we had not been for a while).

A C-17 Globemaster flew us into Honiara. The C-27s arrived with their crew, maintainers and cargo the next day. We had fitted everything we needed onto one aircraft, which made for a simple insertion. Bottled water was one of the biggest items we took with us (all of the empty bottles had to come home with us as we do not want to be a burden of any kind on the nation we are helping). We took two weeks' worth of ration packs and water each.

Our component of Operation *Lilia* was 14 days long. We were tasked to support the Department of Foreign Affairs and Trade and the Solomon Islands Government to ferry vital COVID-19 supplies from Honiara to the outer islands. We also delivered rice, as the Solomon Islands' logistics chains had been severely disrupted by the pandemic. It was incredible to see every team member – no matter their role – helping to load bags and bags of rice. The medical equipment we delivered included oxygen concentrators. One doctor highlighted that a delivery of five oxygen concentrators to a small medical clinic would increase the number of patients they could help at any one time from one to six.

The pace we worked at was a challenge. The team worked so hard and put in long hours. The environment was hot and stuffy, and was made even more uncomfortable by the requirement to wear facemasks. We did not have a single person get the virus during the operation, which is a testament to the team's professionalism and adherence to the COVID-19 protocols, which included daily tests. We called a 'no-fly day' about halfway through, which gave the team time to rest, refuel and prepare for the next high-tempo day.

The mission was a success; we delivered what we were asked to deliver to the places that needed it. The interactions I had with the Solomon Islands Government and Australian officials were always positive. Everyone was amazed by how quickly the team could pull together to get out what was needed. Talking to the Australian Embassy personnel, the message was loud and clear: everyone was thankful that we were there and that we did what we did.

The highlight of any HADR mission is always the people: both the Aussies doing the job, and the locals. Knowing that Aussies are there to support our neighbours in any way possible just makes me smile. And then hearing of the positive impact we had on the population of the Solomon Islands makes it even more special. We are always ready to help. I think it's the Aussie nature.[34]

Leading Aircraftman Sam Schmidt

Royal Australian Air Force

Leading Aircraftman Sam Schmidt marshalling a RAAF C-17 Globemaster at Honiara International Airport in the Solomon Islands during Operation *Lilia* in 2022 (Defence)

Providing HADR support to our Pacific neighbours is equivalent to taking the bins out or checking the mail for one of your neighbours while they're away or not feeling well. It's part of our identity as Australians to help others in times of need.[35]

Mission: COVID-19 support during Operation *Lilia*, 2022

Leading Aircraftman Sam Schmidt helped to transport much-needed supplies to the Solomon Islands following an outbreak of COVID-19 in the island nation.

I first became aware of the COVID-19 support mission to the Solomon Islands when the commanding officer of our squadron, No 382 Squadron, started to ask questions of my section (logistics). These questions related to what it would take to deploy as part of the eventual operation. Because my squadron's role is to deploy at short notice, I was tasked very early on in the planning stage. In terms of official notice, we had two days before we deployed; unofficially, our squadron knew we might be deploying as part of Operation *Lilia* three or four days before we departed the country.

My role during the planning stage involved helping the logistics section to pack and transport the equipment and supplies we needed to deploy. We ensured equipment was serviceable and we had enough food and water to take with us for the duration of the deployment. At this point, we didn't know exactly how long we were going to be deployed for; there was mention of being away from Australia for up to three months.

We had two C-27J Spartans force assigned to the operation; they flew to the Solomon Islands a few days after we had flown over in a C-17A Globemaster with an accompanying C-130J Hercules. These two large Air Mobility Group aircraft were used in conjunction with each other because some of the cargo required for sustained aircraft operations is considered dangerous goods, and therefore isn't able to be transported on the same aircraft as passengers. The two Spartans provided our air-mobility function while we were in the country. During the operation, we also received sustainment flights from Australia in the form of Globemasters delivering extra cargo, COVID-19 health supplies and personal protection equipment for us to distribute to the islands. All personnel deployed on the operation worked in small, highly effective teams to achieve the mission outcome. To support the personnel and mission, we had members providing main capability functions such as command and control, airfield operations, security, medical and air movements. We even deployed with a plumber!

We flew to Honiara International Airport directly from RAAF Amberley in Queensland on a Globemaster; the flight took approximately three hours. During the flight, I spent some time looking out of the windows. I saw some islands so small you probably wouldn't be able to find them on Google Maps. Everyone on the aircraft spent their time calming their minds and doing what they needed to prepare themselves for when we landed and started executing the mission.

The HADR mission was a multi-day task involving transporting cargo from a central hub airport (Honiara International Airport) to smaller airports around the country. Once delivered to the airports, the locals took over the distribution process and delivered the supplies to medical facilities around the islands. To achieve this, we first had to unload all of the cargo from the Globemaster and Hercules and convert the VIP lounge at the airport into our command post. Our cargo also included equipment for the Spartan maintainers to keep their aircraft serviceable throughout the operation. Once all of this was complete, the two Spartans landed in the Solomon Islands and we could begin the mission.

My role during the mission was to provide the air movements functionality for the command post. With the help of other members of the operation, I loaded aircraft two, three or four times a day with thousands of pounds of cargo each time. We ensured all cargo was in compliance with relevant loading publications and that any dangerous goods were packed in accordance with International Air Transport Association guidelines. From the planning stage to deploying to the Solomon Islands and subsequently redeploying back to Australia, I was involved for five to six weeks.

The most challenging part of Operation *Lilia* was the long hours we worked. Most mornings would start just after the sun had risen and would end well after the sun had set most nights. There was lots of heavy lifting and 'playing games of Tetris' to load all of the cargo which we were transporting around to the islands. Additionally, members were then flying with the cargo and offloading thousands of pounds of cargo in very small groups.

The people of the Solomon Islands brought us stories of gratitude and thankfulness from the remote communities. They told us how some of the hospitals were running out of (or had already run out of) the personal protection equipment just as our aircraft were landing. The impact we made while we were there was noticed and felt in the atmosphere. It was incredibly fulfilling to hear stories from the people of the Solomon Islands about the impact we had made. We all felt very welcome during our time in the country and took the tiny amount of free time we had to experience life on the islands. Some of us had the chance to meet locals who operated market stalls and do small procurement shops in the city.

Working in Defence sometimes means you get pushed harder than you ever have been before, see things other people will never get to see, and do things that are bigger than just yourself. In my first two years of working for Defence, I've had more once-in-a-lifetime experiences than I can count with both hands! One week I could be working at my desk in Australia and the next week I could be overseas, loading aircraft and delivering critical supplies to provide humanitarian assistance.

HADR missions are an important part of what we do in Defence because they help to build and strengthen relationships between allied nations. Providing HADR support to our Pacific neighbours is equivalent to taking the bins out or checking the mail for one of your neighbours while they're away or not feeling well. It's part of our identity as Australians to help others in times of need. These missions help to build and foster positive working relationships between countries.[36]

Allies (including the United Kingdom, United States and Australia) to pressure the civilians into switching allegiance. After the Soviet Union blocked roads, railways and waterways leading into Berlin, thereby cutting off their supply lines, the Allies resupplied civilians via thousands of airborne deliveries.[37] As Australia's contribution to the joint mission *Berlin Airlift*, 41 RAAF personnel completed 2,062 deliveries of relief supplies via Douglas C-47 Skytrain (Dakota) aircraft, which were provided by the United Kingdom's Royal Air Force.[38] By the end of 1949, the Soviet Union realised the Allies could supply Berlin indefinitely and so it removed the blockade.[39]

Royal Air Force Douglas C-47 Skytrain (Dakota) aircraft at Berlin Tegel Airport in Germany in 1948 (Wikimedia Commons)

More recently, after a 7.6-magnitude earthquake in Pakistan in 2005 killed at least 86,000 people, injured 69,000 people and displaced 2.8 million more, the ADF delivered desperately needed relief supplies through Operation *Pakistan Assist I*. In just one sub-operation of this multifaceted HADR mission, Operation *Bushranger*, the Army used Sikorsky Black Hawk helicopters to distribute relief supplies to remote villages in the mountains of Pakistan.[40]

An Australian Army Black Hawk preparing to deliver relief supplies to remote mountain villages in Pakistan during Operation *Bushranger* in 2005 (Defence)

In the same region of the world, a magnitude-7.8 earthquake in Nepal in 2015 toppled multistorey buildings in the capital city, Kathmandu, and triggered landslides in the Himalayas, killing nearly 9,000 people.[41] During Operation *Nepal Assist*, the RAAF delivered 154 tonnes of relief supplies via two C-17 Globemasters.[42] Majella Hurney from World Vision Australia explained the shelter kits that made up part of the delivery were especially welcome:

> So many homes and buildings have been destroyed and people are sleeping out in the open. With the monsoon coming in five weeks, there's a real need to make sure there's appropriate shelter.[43]

When humanitarian crises occur in far distant parts of the world, the extra distance from Australia means air power is especially valuable to enable the delivery of relief supplies as quickly as possible. During the South Sudanese Civil War, which started in 2013, thousands of civilians were killed and more than a million were displaced from their homes.[44] Despite the vast distance from Australia to South Sudan, a landlocked country in Africa, the RAAF deployed a C-17 and a C-130J on Operation *Aslan*.[45] Over multiple flights, the aircraft delivered 200 tonnes of supplies to support civilians and United Nations (UN) workers, including generators, water purifiers, tents and body armour.[46]

UN officials and South Sudanese ground personnel help to offload a container of relief supplies from a RAAF C-17 at Juba International Airport in South Sudan during Operation *Aslan* in 2014 (Defence)

Within Australia

While the ADF most frequently delivers relief supplies to foreign nations, at times it delivers them to communities in need within Australia's borders. When Australia itself experiences a disaster – and this large continent with its varied terrain and climates experiences many – the Australian Government meets its duty of care to its own people and visitors from overseas. The RAN's largest HADR mission to date was in Australian territory. Category 4 Cyclone *Tracy* killed 71 people and either destroyed or seriously damaged more than 80% of the buildings in Darwin in the Northern Territory when it struck the city on Christmas Day 1974.[47] During Operation *Navy Help Darwin*, the RAN deployed 13 ships, 11 aircraft and 3,000 personnel to the battered city. The first of these assets to arrive in Darwin were two Hawker Siddeley HS748 aircraft with a delivery of urgently needed blood-transfusion equipment.[48]

A RAN Westland Wessex 31B helicopter delivering relief supplies via a makeshift helipad following Cyclone *Tracy* in 1974. During Operation *Navy Help Darwin*, the RAN deployed aircraft and ships to the devastated city, including the aircraft carrier HMAS *Melbourne*, seen in the background (National Archives of Australia)

Yet, despite the destructiveness of Cyclone *Tracy*, it was far from being the most powerful cyclone to ever have hit Australia. Severe Tropical Cyclone *Yasi* in 2011 holds the dubious record of Australia's largest tropical storm since European settlement.[49] After the Category 5 cyclone made landfall in Queensland, the RAAF operated multiple relief flights via C-17 and C-130 aircraft.[50] Through Operation *Yasi Assist*, it delivered 322 tonnes of relief supplies to the most-affected communities in northern Queensland.[51] More recently, after Ex-Tropical Cyclone *Ellie* caused widespread destruction and flooding throughout Western Australia in early 2023, the state's Department of Fire and Emergency Services requested urgent assistance from the ADF. RAAF Globemaster, Hercules and Spartan aircraft deployed along with Army Taipan and Chinook helicopters to deliver relief supplies to regional and remote communities.[52] Fitzroy Crossing local Natalie Davey recalled:

> We were in crisis and from [the] first community meetings knew that we needed help from Defence because of their training and capability. People needed to know that they were safe and that things could be sorted quickly.[53]

II. Commercial airlines delivering relief supplies

While the ADF has historically played Australia's largest role in delivering relief supplies via air during HADR missions, it has not been the only provider of this critical activity. Australia's commercial airlines – most notably Qantas, the flag carrier of Australia – also have a long history of delivering relief supplies.

To our neighbours

Similarly to the ADF, the majority of commercial airlines' flights to deliver relief supplies have been to our neighbours within the Asia–Pacific region. While Qantas – Australia's longest-running airline with the largest fleet – has contributed more to Australia's HADR efforts than any other commercial airline, Ansett Australia (1936–2002) was involved in an early mission in the Asia–Pacific. After a magnitude-8.1 earthquake hit the Solomon Islands in 1977, Ansett delivered 50 eight-to-10-person tents, which had been donated by the Army, to provide temporary accommodation for civilians whose homes had been destroyed.[56]

After a disaster occurs in a location to which they regularly fly, commercial airlines will frequently provide HADR to the affected nation by filling spare space in their cargo holds with relief supplies. In just one example, after the 2002 Bali bombings in Indonesia, which killed 202 people including 88 Australians, Qantas assisted the large-scale international HADR effort by delivering medical supplies to Bali via multiple scheduled flights.[57] But commercial airlines also often operate dedicated relief flights to help deliver supplies as quickly as possible. Following the Boxing Day tsunami in 2004, Qantas operated dedicated relief flights to Thailand, Sri Lanka and The Maldives to rapidly deliver urgently needed medical equipment.[58]

Around the globe

Just as the ADF does not limit itself to only helping our neighbours, Qantas has similarly delivered relief supplies to destinations far beyond the Asia–Pacific region. An early example also demonstrates the generosity of Qantas employees. For a decade following the Second World War, a prolonged period of extreme cold weather, combined with a national commitment to export food to war-torn Europe, led the United Kingdom to enforce stricter food rationing on its citizens than it had during the war.[59] To provide some relief to the hungry nation, on Qantas's inaugural Sydney-to-London flight in 1947, its Lockheed Constellation *Charles Kingsford Smith* carried nearly a tonne of food parcels which had been donated by Qantas employees.[60]

Qantas Constellation *Charles Kingsford Smith* carrying food parcels on its inaugural flight from Sydney to London in 1947 to help offset the United Kingdom's strict post-war rationing (Qantas)

Warrant Officer Shaunn Segon

Royal Australian Air Force

Loadmaster Warrant Officer Shaunn Segon securing a load in a RAAF C-27J Spartan (Defence)

It's never good to see people in distress or needing help, but when they are in need, we are ready to move.[54]

Mission: Ex-Tropical Cyclone *Ellie*, 2023

Warrant Officer Shaunn Segon helped to deliver essential supplies to regional Western Australia following Ex-Tropical Cyclone Ellie *in 2023.*

Undertaking any HADR task is extremely satisfying, in that we are directly helping fellow Australians or our neighbours when they are in need. It's never good to see people in distress or needing help, but when they are in need, we are ready to move.

Our No 35 Squadron crews are placed on a programmed standby ready for call out well before the Christmas break, and we always watch the news to gain a heads-up on where we may need to go if we're on the hook to be called. From this, we have a good communications plan, with crews on 12-hours' and 24-hours' notice to move: bags packed, equipment ready, and our families prepared. Leaving families is always hard during the Christmas holidays, especially for those with young children, but the kids understand what we do and they always try to watch the news to catch a glimpse of Mum or Dad when they're away on operations. Prior to this mission, I had volunteered to hold the call out during the Christmas and new year period as my kids are a little older now, and it gives the younger families a chance to enjoy Christmas without being called into work.

I was involved very early on for this particular call out and worked closely with my detachment commander to ensure that we had all of the gear necessary for a multitude of contingencies, as there were a lot of unknowns – were we going to carry passengers and cargo, or conduct airdrop of supplies, or do aeromedical evacuations? – so we had to ensure that all of the necessary gear was packed on the aircraft.

Everyone pitches in to ensure that we have everything we need: the maintenance crew bring all of the spare parts we may need and their toolkits, the pilots ensure that all charts and planning equipment for the mission are ready, and the loadmasters collect all of the necessary loading equipment, then load and secure everything into the C-27J Spartan. Loadmasters are sometimes known as Tetris champions: shoehorning all of the equipment into the aircraft and ensuring that it's all restrained and that the aircraft is within its flying limits.

The variety of loads we carry make it a great challenge sometimes. We need to work out if the load can safely be carried, with respect to making sure it's restrained correctly and is within the aircraft's centre-of-gravity limits. Time constraints can be a big player: in Broome in Western Australia following Ex-Tropical Cyclone *Ellie*, we had a two-hour window to have the loads out of the refrigerated truck and loaded onto the aircraft, then we had to fly to Derby, land, and then unload the cargo into another refrigerated truck. With the flying time running at around 30 minutes, that left 45 minutes to load and 45 minutes to unload. We met all of the time windows with a five- to 15-minute buffer. The cargo we carried was mainly fresh fruit and vegetables and frozen food for resupplying the local supermarket so people could get food. We carried about six tonnes of food on each flight, normally flying two to three shuttles per aircraft each day.

What made it a little more challenging was the heat and humidity: lathered in sweat with our flying suits sticking to us made moving around the loads and aircraft difficult. We usually rested up during the short flights and tried to rehydrate and grab a bite to eat.

As well as transporting supplies, during this mission we also moved displaced people whose homes had flooded, or transported critical personnel such as doctors. We even carried a dog belonging to one of the doctors who was stranded in Derby! The dog wasn't too afraid of the aircraft noise once we got her on board. The local kids were great to carry; they were well behaved and because the Spartan climbs like a rocket, they all got a bit of a surprise by the take-off climb rate and thought it was a roller coaster; they were whooping and yelling and all smiling and having a great time!

Australia has the resources, experience and expertise to help when we are called upon to do so. Getting involved in HADR missions shows that we as Australians and as members of the ADF are willing and able to help. It doesn't matter what religion or race you may be, what political views or past experiences you may have, we will assist you to the best of our ability when we are tasked by our government. This builds friendships and trust at a personal, group and government level.[55]

More recently, in 2021, the Australian Government chartered a Qantas flight to transport more than a thousand ventilators and dozens of oxygen concentrators to India to help treat those suffering from COVID-19 at the peak of the pandemic.[61] Australia's foreign minister at the time, Marise Payne, noted India's contribution to battling the global pandemic through the development of vaccines, acknowledging those who provide help may also need help in turn:

> India has shown great leadership and generosity to the world in exporting vaccines globally. It is time for the world to repay that generosity and Australia as a close friend of the Indian people is playing its part.[62]

Urgently needed ventilators being loaded onto a Qantas flight bound for India in 2021 (Prime Minister's Office)

Within Australia

Back home, Qantas is well positioned to deliver relief supplies to almost every corner of Australia via its regular scheduled services. The smaller aircraft in the regional QantasLink fleet means Qantas can also operate scheduled or dedicated relief flights to smaller airfields which are closer to the disaster location or which cannot be used by its larger aircraft. This enables Qantas additional capacity to engage in HADR in remote areas. Occasionally, the relief supplies on board the aircraft are urgently needed to help contain a disaster even as it unfolds. A recent example is from Australia's horrific bushfire season of 2019–20, which killed 34 people and destroyed more than 46 million acres of land as well as homes, infrastructure and crops.[63] As the fires burned out of control, Qantas delivered tonnes of firefighting equipment around the nation to assist with the firefighting effort.

III. Airdropping relief supplies

When conditions on the ground during a humanitarian crisis mean an aircraft cannot safely land to deliver relief supplies – for example, if a tsunami or cyclone has badly damaged the only runway on an island – then the ADF may deploy its aircraft and crew on an airdrop mission.[64] Airdrops involve releasing a parachute of supplies from an aircraft, with the aim of it landing within an acceptable range of an ideal target site.[65] The RAAF most frequently uses its C-17 Globemaster, C-130 Hercules and C-27 Spartan aircraft for airdrop missions: each type has a ramp which can be opened mid-flight.

The complex physical interplay between cargo weight, aircraft altitude and speed, wind speed, parachute drag and so on – which has historically limited the chances the supplies will hit the target site, let alone in good condition – is less of a contributing factor to the success of Australia's airdrop missions since the ADF adopted the joint precision airdrop system.[66] This system uses steerable parachutes and global positioning system (GPS) technology to improve the accuracy of airdrops.[67] During a proof-of-concept flight for the joint precision airdrop system in 2015, the RAAF released an 800-kilogram load at high altitude from a C-130 Hercules, approximately 18.5 kilometres from the target site in the Woomera Test Range in South Australia.[68] Flight Lieutenant Jason Della Bosca from the Air Movements Training and Development Unit reported: 'The load landed within 25 metres from the planned point of impact, and within six seconds of [the] predicted flight time.'[69]

A RAAF C-27J Spartan dropping a supply bundle during airdrop training near RAAF Base Richmond in New South Wales in 2020 (Defence)

A greater challenge during HADR airdrop missions is the lack of military presence on the ground to oversee the handover of the cargo to local responsible parties increases the chances they will not be distributed as intended. This means if no one – or if an irresponsible or corrupt party – takes charge of the relief supplies once they are on the ground, then those who are most in need may never receive them.[70] Despite this risk, airdrop is sometimes the ADF's best, or only, option to deliver relief supplies. This is often the case during times of conflict. The ADF's airdrop mission during Operation *Okra* is a recent example of a successful delivery of aid in a dangerous situation. The Islamic State of Iraq and the Levant (ISIS) seized the city of Sinjar and surrounding villages in Iraq in 2014, murdering 5,000 members of the local Yazidi population and abducting hundreds more.[71] Surviving Yazidis fled to nearby Mount Sinjar where they endured searing temperatures for days with no water or food.[72] In response to this humanitarian crisis, the Australian Government tasked the ADF to urgently deliver relief supplies. The RAAF rapidly deployed to Iraq and airdropped nine tonnes of supplies via C-130J Hercules to the Yazidi refugees on Mount Sinjar, including sufficient water and high-energy biscuits to sustain 3,700 people for 24 hours.[73] Operation *Okra* was unusual (although not unique), in that air power was used to both deliver HADR (via cargo aircraft) as well as combat the violence that contributed to the need for HADR (via combat aircraft). The *Stabilisation and Humanitarian Operations* doctrine confirms: 'The majority of HADR activities are non-warlike operations. However, HADR may be conducted in the presence of some form of conflict.'[74] During Operation *Okra*:

> In addressing the growing humanitarian crisis, and potential genocide, the US-led coalition had to rely upon air power to respond with air strikes against Islamic State forces and air mobility to deliver critically needed supplies to the embattled Yazidis.[75]

Fifteen pallets of relief supplies in a RAAF C-130J Hercules prior to being airdropped to Yazidi refugees on Mount Sinjar in Iraq during Operation *Okra* in 2014 (Defence)

The crew of a RAAF Hercules preparing to airdrop relief supplies to Yazidi refugees on Mount Sinjar (Defence)

Chapter 2
EVACUATION AND AEROMEDICAL EVACUATION

In addition to the delivery and airdrop of relief supplies, one of the most common uses of Australian air power in humanitarian aid and disaster relief (HADR) missions is the evacuation of injured or vulnerable people. Both the Australian Defence Force (ADF) and Qantas are involved in evacuation missions in accordance with their capabilities and the circumstances of the disaster.

Evacuations can include aeromedical evacuations, which in ideal situations use aircraft such as the C-27J Spartan which can be configured to carry hospital-grade medical facilities and medical personnel to treat passengers inflight. For this reason, it is usually – although not always – the ADF rather than commercial airlines that provides Australia's aeromedical-evacuation capability.

I. The Australian Defence Force providing evacuation and aeromedical evacuation

To our neighbours

As a truly multicultural people with strong ties to other countries, it is not surprising Australians are caught up in foreign conflicts from time to time. As a result, the Australian Government often tasks the ADF to evacuate Australian citizens from foreign conflict zones. Yet, in line with its mission to be a good international citizen that cares for the rights of all humans, Australia will also often evacuate non-Australian nationals from conflict zones. Against the backdrop of dangerous and rapidly escalating violence and war, the ADF most often uses air power for its evacuation missions, to both get to the affected nation, and get away again with the evacuees safely on board, as quickly as possible.

The ADF was involved in one of the most famous airborne-evacuation missions in history: Operation *Babylift*. By the end of the decades-long Vietnam War in 1975, millions of civilians and soldiers from both sides of the conflict were dead.[1] Following the collapse of the South Vietnamese government, while North Vietnamese troops were en route to the capital city of South Vietnam, Australia joined the United States and other allied nations in evacuating an estimated 3,300 orphans of war from Saigon. Many of these required medical care while inflight. During Operation *Babylift*, the Royal Australian Air Force (RAAF) evacuated 194 orphans to Bangkok in Thailand; all were babies or small children, and many travelled in cardboard boxes on the floor of two C-130 Hercules aircraft.[2] RAAF nursing officer Phyllis Schumann recalled:

> Awaiting us were two C-130 Hercules aircraft with engines running, into which all the children had already been loaded. We nurses were assisted up the loading ramp of the second C-130 as it started taxiing to the runway. The pilots were most apprehensive as parts of the airfield were under attack. On board, it was very hot and noisy. There were webbing seats running along either side of the aircraft, which was not configured for a medical-evacuation mission. Confusion reigned for a while until everyone sorted things out. We were able to comfort the terrified children, who had never experienced the inside of a large military transport aircraft. Initially, we were intent on getting fluids into the orphans as quickly as possible, as they were obviously very dehydrated. Intravenous lines and fluids were used in the worst cases.[3]

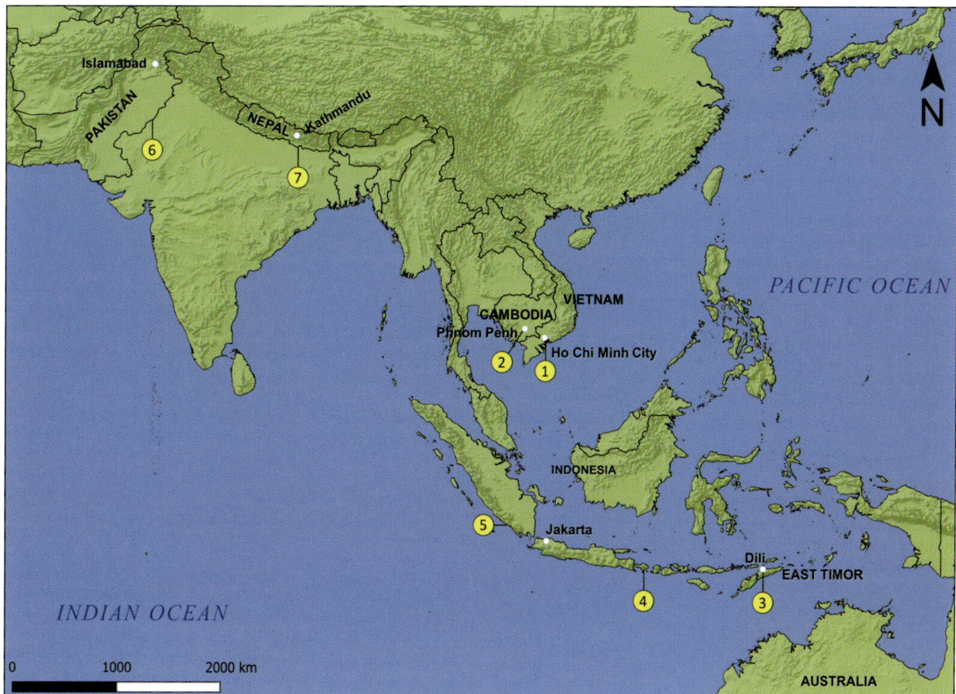

Selected Australian Defence Force evacuation and aeromedical evacuation missions: Asia–Pacific

1. Operation *Babylift*, Vietnam, 1975
2. Operation *Vista*, Cambodia, 1997
3. Operation *Spitfire*, East Timor, 1999
4. Operation *Bali Assist*, Indonesia, 2002
5. Operation *Sumatra Assist II*, Indonesia, 2005
6. Operation *Pakistan Assist I*, 2005–06
7. Operation *Nepal Assist*, 2015

RAAF personnel caring for Vietnamese orphans of war during Operation *Babylift* in 1975 (Defence)

Concurrently to Operation *Babylift*, the RAAF also evacuated 80 Australians, predominantly embassy officials and their families who lived in Saigon, before North Vietnamese troops arrived in the city.[4] This evacuation mission predated a similar one in neighbouring Cambodia two decades later. After the United Nations Transitional Authority in Cambodia withdrew from the nation in 1997, the Cambodian People's Party staged a coup, which led to widespread violence and compelled Australians and other foreign nationals to evacuate the country.[5] The fighting was especially violent in the capital city, Phnom Penh, and around its international airport, Pochentong Airport, thereby making it difficult for people to leave.[6] Despite the significant risks to its personnel and aircraft, the RAAF rapidly deployed on Operation *Vista*. In a single day, the RAAF evacuated 454 Australian, New Zealand and Canadian citizens from Pochentong Airport via four C-130 Hercules aircraft.[7] A similar occasion which demanded a rapid evacuation from a conflict zone was during East Timor's fight for independence in 1999. During Operation *Spitfire*, as soldiers from Indonesia's military and paramilitary murdered 2,000 East Timorese citizens, the ADF evacuated 2,478 Australians and foreign nationals via C-130.[8]

When critically injured people must be evacuated from a disaster location, the speed of the mission is even more crucial if their lives are to be saved. In such situations, air power truly demonstrates its value. Within little more than half a day – just 13 hours – of the 2002 Bali bombings, the ADF had embarked on Operation *Bali Assist*, evacuating 66 seriously and critically injured patients to Australia.[9]

While evacuees are most frequently fleeing from locations which have experienced conflict, such as terrorism or war, the ADF will also evacuate people from the sites of natural disasters. The reasons for evacuating people in these situations may vary: dangerous effects of the natural disaster may be ongoing (for example, aftershocks following an earthquake), or their departure may ease the burden on the affected country as it attempts to restore critical infrastructure and services, or they may simply have no other way of leaving the country due to the cancellation of outbound travel. After Category 5 Severe Tropical Cyclone *Pam* killed dozens of people in the South Pacific in 2015, the RAAF evacuated 199 Australians to Brisbane via two C-17s and a C-130.[10] Australian citizen Liliui Okalani Botleng, who had been stranded in Vanuatu along with her family following the cyclone, observed: 'The Royal Australian Air Force is doing a very good job and are very helpful. I am able to go home because of them.'[11] Also in 2015, after the magnitude-7.8 Gorkha earthquake killed nearly 9,000 people in Nepal, the ADF embarked on Operation *Nepal Assist*. A C-17 and its crew evacuated more than 100 tourists and volunteer workers, including 66 Australians, from Kathmandu in Nepal to Bangkok in Thailand.[12]

A group of Australians passing the time with a game of cards in a RAAF C-17 Globemaster as they evacuate from Kathmandu to Bangkok during Operation *Nepal Assist* in 2015 (Defence)

The earlier examples of the evacuation missions out of Cambodia and East Timor referred to the significant safety risks inherent in such missions. It is a sad reality that, on rare occasions, evacuation or aeromedical-evacuation missions which aim to save lives tragically claim them instead. The ADF deployed on Operation *Sumatra Assist II* in response to the devastating

2005 Nias–Simeulue earthquake which struck Indonesia only three months after the Boxing Day tsunami in 2004. Sadly, while en route to the island of Nias to evacuate severely injured locals, *Shark 02*, a Royal Australian Navy (RAN) Westland Sea King helicopter, crashed with a full crew and aeromedical-evacuation team, killing six RAN and three RAAF personnel.[13]

Around the globe

Selected Australian Defence Force evacuation missions: Middle East/Africa

1. Operation *Ramp*, Lebanon, 2006
2. Operation *Carnelian*, Sudan, 2023

Several Australian airborne-evacuation missions are notable not only for the large number of people who were safely evacuated, but also for taking place a great distance from Australia. One of these was Operation *Ramp* during the 2006 Lebanon War.[14] After Lebanese militant group Hezbollah fired rockets into Israel, and the Israel Defense Forces retaliated by bombing towns and infrastructure in Lebanon, the Australian Government tasked the ADF with a large-scale evacuation of its citizens and allied civilians. The ADF supported the Department of Foreign Affairs and Trade (DFAT) during Operation *Ramp* to evacuate 5,300 Australians and more than 1,300 foreign nationals from the warzone.[15] Former RAAF officer Graeme O'Brien observed:

> Operation *Ramp* can only be considered as an outstanding success. The distance from home, the large number of evacuees and the liaison required for safe passage within war-torn Lebanon and neighbouring countries made *Ramp* an extremely complex operation.[16]

Wing Commander Innis checking on Australian nationals evacuating from Lebanon via a RAAF C-130J Hercules during Operation *Ramp* in 2006 (Defence)

A more recent example of an ADF evacuation mission a long way from Australia was, in fact, the largest airborne-evacuation mission in recent history. In August 2021, the Taliban moved to regain control of Afghanistan, thereby placing many civilians and foreign nationals at great risk. The global response was an allied coalition evacuation mission. For Australia, in coordination with DFAT and the Department of Home Affairs, the ADF deployed five aircraft and the Army's Ready Combat Team to evacuate 4,100 Australians along with some foreign nationals – aged from just eight days to 81 years – from Kabul to Australia's main operating base in the Middle East. The pace was high tempo, with one RAAF C-17 evacuating

Squadron Leader Kevin Auld

Royal Australian Air Force

Kevin Auld (then a sergeant) helps to settle Australian evacuees from Lebanon into a RAAF Hercules during Operation *Ramp* in 2006 (Defence)

Everyone we evacuated was met with an Australian flag and an Aussie wanting to help. Every civilian we evacuated was grateful; their emotions varied from being relieved to being overwhelmed. A number of people continually thanked us and some of us got a few hugs![17]

Mission: Operation *Ramp*, 2006

Squadron Leader Kevin Auld was involved in Operation Ramp, *the ADF's evacuation mission during the 2006 Lebanon War.*

I first became aware Defence was planning an HADR mission in support of Operation *Ramp* when I received a phone call at about 2am from my flight commander, stating we had a planning meeting with Headquarters Air Lift Group (now Air Movements Group) the next day. It was my role to advise the online aircraft security team that we had a potential task with short notice to move. All members were directed to report at 7am the next morning and be prepared to travel that day. At this point, we had no idea what the task was or where we may go.

The initial scoping my flight commander and I were involved in was based around how many people we may need to secure a C-130 Hercules which would need to transit through a number of airfields. After the initial conversations around the numbers of people required, a large portion of my effort then shifted to making sure we had the correct equipment and that our pre-deployment paperwork and checks were still current. The timeframe between that 2am phone call and departing Australia was about two-and-a-half days.

Our planning in Australia was very fluid because the conflict between Israel and Lebanon was still unfolding and our role was still being developed. Our unit planning was focused on getting there and being flexible; we did assume we would be helping to move Australians out of Lebanon. The RAAF contingent consisted of two parts: the C-130 crew (including the Airfield Defence Squadron Aircraft Security Team) and the Expeditionary Contingency Support Squadron (ECSS). Our deployment to Cyprus was through a contracted civilian air provider; from there we transferred to the C-130 with the crew and flew into Royal Air Force (RAF) Akrotiri in Cyprus. I distinctly remember our arrival in Akrotiri as it was the first time I'd ever seen a United States Air Force U-2 aircraft, which took off not long after we had landed.

The initial plan to have us housed at RAF Akrotiri had fallen through by the time we arrived. The C-130 crew left for a hotel in the city of Larnika while the rest of us were left to sleep in the boatshed on the RAF base. My bed for the first night was an inflatable ring normally towed behind a boat! Luckily, our flight commander was able to get us accommodated with the C-130 crew at the hotel along with the Joint Task Force (JTF) team, who deployed to conduct the operation after the first night.

The entire mission after we arrived took about 16 days. One highlight for me was our planning and rehearsals of how we would transfer evacuees from the port at Tire in Türkiye (Turkey) to a ship anchored away from the port; it involved a lot of dynamic trials of different boarding ladders and transferring people at sea. After about a week, our focus shifted to moving the evacuees out of their hotels and linking them to international flights back to Australia. We moved a number of people to Istanbul Airport in Türkiye via C-130, with them then catching connecting flights via Qantas back to Australia.

As the airfields in Lebanon were damaged and the C-130 couldn't land there, we volunteered to assist the Evacuation Handling Centre at Limassol in Cyprus, which was run by the ECSS. These ended up being long days – more than 20 hours at times – as the evacuation by the JTF was now being conducted using hired vessels between Tire and Limassol. As my team were extras to the ECSS plan, we were flexible and jumped in when we saw areas breaking down or being overwhelmed with people. For instance, when there were issues with media interest impacting injured evacuees, we liaised with the local police and had exclusion zones established. Fatigue crept up on us; before we knew it, we had done five or six 20-hour days in a row. Knowing how to deal with a wave of people who needed reassurance and assistance was also initially something completely different for all of us.

From the RAAF's perspective, Operation *Ramp* was about helping Australians in their time of need. Everyone we evacuated was met with an Australian flag and an Aussie wanting to help. Every civilian we evacuated was grateful; their emotions varied from being relieved to being overwhelmed. A number of people continually thanked us and some of us got a few hugs! I have a clear memory of talking to a family who were waiting to be processed by RAAF members who were assisting the Department of Foreign Affairs and Trade; they were thanking me for my assistance repeatedly and it left me feeling very humble.

HADR missions to me are about the humanity all of us have in being a part of the RAAF and ADF. They help to centre us, in that they are the opposite of the effect we train and exist for: we get to focus purely on helping others and hopefully making a positive difference.[18]

350 people on a single flight, and a RAAF KC-30A Multi-Role Tanker Transport refuelling coalition fast jets mid-air to maintain the security of the airspace during the evacuation. Sadly, during the United States's series of evacuations, 13 United States military personnel lost their lives.[19] Air Commodore David Paddison, Commander of the ADF's Joint Task Force, noted, 'While there are stories of tragedy, Australian Defence personnel should be proud of their contribution to either return people home or give others a new start.'[20]

Another recent evacuation mission from a conflict zone – which also represented genuine risk to the men and women who flew in to help evacuate their fellow Australians – took place in 2023. When fighting broke out in Sudan between the Sudanese Armed Forces and the paramilitary group Rapid Support Forces, foreign nationals were exposed to violence. The ADF embarked on the evacuation mission Operation *Carnelian*, which was led by DFAT and involved officials from Home Affairs and Australian Border Force (ABF). During two flights, RAAF C-130Js evacuated 153 Australians and foreign nationals from Sudan to Cyprus.[21] Australia's foreign minister, Penny Wong, observed: 'That is a good outcome. We're pleased that that's happened safely in what is quite a difficult security situation.'[22]

Even though the RAAF, with its readily configurable aircraft, has the best aeromedical-evacuation capabilities of the three ADF services, the circumstances of the disaster sometimes mean the RAN or Army are better equipped or physically located to conduct the mission. Contributing factors can include aircraft availability, such as when the Army and its aircraft have already deployed to a location near the disaster, and environmental conditions, such as when no runways are available for fixed-wing aircraft to land. These factors contributed to the ADF's evacuation mission following the catastrophic Kashmir earthquake in Pakistan in 2005. During Operation *Pakistan Assist I*, the Army conducted 42 aeromedical-evacuation flights via Sikorsky Black Hawk helicopters.[25]

Within Australia

The Australian Government also frequently tasks the ADF to provide evacuation and aeromedical-evacuation missions within our own borders. In Australia's largest-ever peacetime evacuation, 35,362 people (out of a population of approximately 47,000) evacuated Darwin following Cyclone *Tracy* in 1974.[26] The ADF's contribution to this large-scale evacuation effort was 9,678 people. Approximately 600 of these were patients whom the RAAF evacuated on aeromedical-evacuation flights to southern cities for medical treatment.[27] Much more recently, but again in the Northern Territory, after persistent rain in the Top End in early 2023, the ADF assisted local emergency services with evacuating civilians from isolated communities on the flooded Victoria River. The RAAF deployed two C-130J Hercules and a C-27J Spartan aircraft on multiple flights between RAAF Base Tindal near Katherine and the flooded communities, to evacuate around 600 people.[28]Aircraftman Daniel Shaw, who was involved in the mission during his first posting in the RAAF, reflected:

> Being involved in a tasking like this is such a rewarding experience. I am so grateful of having the experience to help out the people affected by this terrible disaster. My involvement makes me proud to put on the [RAAF] uniform.[29]

Sergeant Jacquelyn Nelson

Royal Australian Air Force

The passengers were kind, excited and seemed surprisingly optimistic given the dire circumstances they had just come from. It was rewarding to be a part of this HADR mission and I remain honoured to have served alongside my ADF and whole-of-government teammates.[23]

Mission: Operation *Carnelian*, 2023

Sergeant Jacquelyn Nelson was involved in Operation Carnelian, *the evacuation of Australians and allied civilians from Sudan in 2023.*

I first became aware Defence was planning an HADR mission in support of Operation *Carnelian* when my operations warrant officer called me upstairs to ask if I had been inoculated against yellow fever. I had been, so I was told to immediately pack my bags for Sudan.

I was just about to wind down from a busy six-day work week when the task came in. The team was given 18 hours' notice to move, so I immediately commenced preparing our fly-away kit and making contact with the aircrew to anticipate what equipment we would need to complete the mission. I contacted Joint Operations Command and all of the air movements sections I anticipated we would require support from on our way over to Sudan. These included RAAF Base Richmond in New South Wales, RAAF Base Learmonth in Western Australia, and the deployed air movements teams at Al Minhad Air Base in the United Arab Emirates.

In the majority of HADR missions, it's the air movements sections around Australia, and at any forward operating bases in the area of operations, that take the brunt of the load. Information changes so quickly that the teams must be flexible and reactive, and the pallet-building process and loading priorities can change multiple times before the aircraft's wheels leave the runway. RAAF Amberley's air movements section in Queensland can be given tasks which may include weeks, days or just hours of pallet building, operational planning and physical loading. Teams will also be tasked to accompany the cargo and assist with the offloading and distribution once in the area of operations.

Air movements is a highly responsive mustering which constantly conducts contingency planning and preparation for the broad range of tasks we may be called upon to support. These may include refuelling, running the passenger terminal, connecting ground power, load planning, accepting dangerous goods including explosive ordnance, and building and loading/unloading Australian and foreign aircraft – to name a few! Cargo may include vehicles, helicopters, tanks, weapons, submarines, HADR stores and medical supplies, heavy machinery (such as forklifts), and general cargo such as personnel baggage, food and even animals.

The Operation *Carnelian* HADR mission commenced on 27 April 2023 and concluded on 12 May 2023, and I was involved from start to finish. Due to the small number of people in my immediate team who were tasked to service both C-130 missions (four ADF members, including myself), fatigue was our greatest risk. Our longest working day was 19 hours and our shortest was eight hours. Our days of flying included the preparation of cargo before and after each task, along with the refurbishment of the aircraft to assist the loadmasters.

We departed for Sudan from RAAF Amberley in Queensland. After my team and I next arrived at RAAF Base Richmond, we assisted No 22 Squadron Air Movements to build and load two C-130 Hercules aircraft. The cargo consisted of aircraft technicians' equipment, personal weapons (due to the potential of civil unrest in the area in which we would be landing) and personnel baggage. We then continued to RAAF Base Learmonth in Western Australia, Diego Garcia in the British Indian Ocean Territory, Al Minhad Air Base in the United Arab Emirates, Cyprus, and finally Port Sudan in Sudan.

During this mission, personnel support consisted of technicians, special forces personnel, airfield-defence guards, mobile air load team personnel (my team), aircrew, and personnel from the ABF and DFAT. The mobile air load team in Al Minhad, led by Flight Sergeant Kenneth Szekely, kindly assisted us after our arrival in Al Minhad because they knew we had worked and travelled for long hours and days to get there.

An Australian government official sitting with evacuees from Sudan on board a RAAF Hercules during Operation *Carnelian* in 2023 (Defence)

Our mission involved evacuating Australian citizens and other foreign nationals from Sudan to Cyprus. My role specifically for this part of the mission was to liaise with the ABF, DFAT and the loadmasters to formulate a workable and safe plan for the transport of the evacuees and their belongings. A highlight of the mission for me was working alongside the loadmasters from No 37 Squadron on all legs of the mission. For this particular task, I also liaised with medical personnel and the special forces members for guidance on what we should do if someone was unwell during a flight, or if a security incident occurred. My team assisted in handing out food and water during the evacuations, and the medical personnel helped anyone on board who required it.

The final outcome of the mission was the safe movement of 153 civilians from Sudan to Cyprus. The passengers were kind, excited and seemed surprisingly optimistic given the dire circumstances they had just come from. It was rewarding to be a part of this HADR mission and I remain honoured to have served alongside my ADF and whole-of-government teammates.[24]

Corporal Deniele Oehm

Royal Australian Air Force

Loadmaster Corporal Deniele Oehm high-fives a young passenger during an evacuation flight in 2023 following Ex-Tropical Cyclone *Ellie* (Defence)

The evacuees were predominantly young children and the elderly, who were unable to leave without help. Even though they had just been through a devastating experience, and were now being told to leave their homes without knowing when they would be able to return, they still had smiles on their faces and were extremely thankful.[35]

Mission: Ex-Tropical Cyclone *Ellie*, 2023

Corporal Deniele Oehm helped to evacuate civilians, and deliver essential personnel and supplies, following Ex-Tropical Cyclone Ellie *in regional Western Australia in 2023.*

I first became aware Defence was planning an HADR mission in Western Australia following Ex-Tropical Cyclone *Ellie* when I was contacted by my chain of command at No 35 Squadron and asked if I would be available during the next week. It was the end of the Christmas period and most people were on leave. After I said I would be available, I was told to pack a bag for roughly five days. I was given less than 48 hours' notice for the task.

The planning stage was very different to our usual tasking as we normally have more notice and more information as to what we will be doing. We didn't know if we would be evacuating people or delivering supplies, so we had to make sure we had all of the required equipment for any mission – which is a lot!

We departed RAAF Amberley in Queensland on a C-27J Spartan and landed in Kununurra in Western Australia approximately 6.5 hours later. Our crew consisted of two pilots, two loadmasters (including myself), one detachment commander, one operations officer and five maintainers.

Our mission involved evacuating locals whose homes had flooded, as well as taking emergency workers, medical professionals and essential food and pharmaceuticals into flood-affected areas. The most challenging aspect for the loadmasters was working out the most efficient and effective way of moving cold loads without them spoiling. This was hard work in humid Broome. The tropical heat and afternoon thunderstorms also resulted in extremely challenging flying and loading conditions. But by the end of the mission, we had successfully evacuated and transported 352 passengers and moved more than 500,000lbs of cargo.

The overall response from the civilians whom we supported was gratitude. In the mornings, we would go to the supermarket in uniform to grab ice and water for the flights, and locals would come up and ask us how it was going and thank us for the hard work we were doing. This was my first HADR mission and it made me realise how much it means to remote communities to have our support.

The highlight of the mission for me was the evacuation of locals from Fitzroy Crossing. The local airfield was submerged and very soft, and the only fixed-wing ADF aircraft that could land was the Spartan. The evacuees were predominantly young children and the elderly, who were unable to leave without help. Even though they had just been through a devastating experience, and were now being told to leave their homes without knowing when they would be able to return, they still had smiles on their faces and were extremely thankful. This made me realise how important what we do is and the impact it has.

This mission was challenging and tested my new skills, but with the support of the experienced loadmaster and every other member of the detachment, it was a highly valuable experience for learning. I felt really good having done something that helped so many people in need.[36]

The ADF is often tasked to evacuate at-risk people who would otherwise be simply unable to leave, often from hospitals and other care facilities. In 2011, as Severe Tropical Cyclone *Yasi* approached the Queensland coast, the RAAF evacuated 173 hospital patients from Cairns to Brisbane.[30] Many of these patients were unable to leave their hospital beds or wheelchairs without assistance and almost all had to be closely monitored for the duration of the flight. Group Captain Don Sutherland stated during Operation *Yasi Assist*: 'When a natural disaster happens or when the government calls us to perform this, we're ready.'[31] Also in Queensland, the ADF was involved in the state's largest mandatory evacuation to date. The 2010–11 Queensland floods affected 200,000 people, caused 33 deaths, and had ongoing effects throughout the state for several years. During Operation *Queensland Flood Assist*, all three ADF services evacuated civilians from rising floodwaters in regional towns, including 32 senior citizens from the town of St George and 90 patients from Bundaberg Hospital.[32]

Able Seaman Anthony Peters assisting residents of Forest Hill in Queensland to prepare to evacuate via a RAN Sea King helicopter during Operation *Queensland Flood Assist* in 2011. In the background, an Army Black Hawk helicopter takes off with other evacuees on board (Defence)

More recently, after Ex-Tropical Cyclone *Ellie* struck Western Australia in early 2023, the RAAF deployed C-27s to assist Western Australia's Department of Communities to evacuate civilians with severe health conditions, along with those who had been left homeless by the flooding.[33] One of the RAAF loadmasters during the evacuation mission, Corporal Deniele Oehm, observed:

> These families are so thankful, and it's great to see the kids so excited. It was just a matter of making them feel comfortable because this was their first time on a military aircraft.[34]

II. Commercial airlines providing evacuation and aeromedical evacuation

According to *The Sydney Morning Herald*, 'Qantas remains the first port of call when the government needs a commercial airline to evacuate Australians.'[37] And in fact, Qantas has risked its aircraft and crewmembers many times to bring home Australians who have been caught up in conflicts and natural disasters overseas.

Qantas will frequently operate dedicated flights to evacuate Australians from foreign disaster zones as rapidly as possible. After the Bali bombings in Indonesia in 2002, the airline evacuated 1,000 Australians, many with serious burns, on five dedicated Boeing 767 flights.[38] Following this initial evacuation, Qantas then operated an additional nine dedicated flights to bring home more than 4,500 Australians from Bali, including many who had tickets for other airlines.[39] Even when Qantas evacuates Australians from conflict zones far beyond the Asia–Pacific region, it will fly them home to Australia at no cost to evacuees. In 2011, protestors triggered an Egyptian revolution when they called for the increasingly despotic President Mubārak to step down.[40] Mubārak and his supporters responded with increasing violence, injuring and killing hundreds of civilians.[41] When Qantas evacuated 400 Australians from the turmoil in Cairo on two Boeing 747 flights, the airline also offered them free onward flights to Australia.[42] Alan Joyce, then chief executive officer of Qantas, reflected: 'It's the right thing to do and we are proud to do it.'[43]

Australian evacuees from Wuhan in China arriving at RAAF Base Learmonth in Western Australia in 2020 (Department of Home Affairs)

Qantas also evacuates Australians who have been affected by natural disasters, both overseas and within Australia. In fact, it was during a domestic evacuation mission in 1974 that Qantas broke a world record. Following Cyclone *Tracy*, the airline evacuated 4,900 people from Darwin, including a record-breaking flight of 674 evacuees plus 23 crewmembers on a single Boeing 747.[44] More recently, following the global attempt to contain the COVID-19 virus, which has killed millions of people around the world, Qantas evacuated hundreds of Australians stranded overseas due to travel restrictions. During the first months of the pandemic in 2020, the airline evacuated 243 Australians from Wuhan in China, where the virus originated; 180 Australians from the cruise ship *Diamond Princess* in the Port of Yokohama in Japan; and hundreds more stranded in countries as varied and widespread as Argentina, Cambodia, India, Nepal, Peru, The Philippines and South Africa.[45]

Only on rare occasions has the Australian Government asked Qantas to evacuate foreign nationals, rather than Australians, from overseas. During the joint mission Operation *Babylift* in 1975, the government chartered a Qantas Boeing 747 to evacuate some of the sickest of the Vietnamese orphans of war from Bangkok in Thailand to Australia.[46] RAAF nursing officer Phyllis Schumann recalled:

> On arrival in Bangkok, we all transferred to the Qantas 747, which was ready for the long haul to Melbourne. We used cardboard cartons as improvised cots for the babies. Every available space in the aircraft was soon filled to capacity, with the very sick orphans placed to the rear of the aircraft to receive intensive nursing. The Qantas staff were extremely helpful in keeping up a 'fluids and nappy patrol' throughout the aircraft. Nearing Melbourne, we dressed the orphans in extra clothing, anticipating the cooler weather: it was eight degrees! On arrival at Tullamarine in the early morning, amid tight security, the very ill children were transferred first to waiting ambulances.[47]

During Operation *Babylift*, Qantas evacuated 215 refugees, all babies and small children, who were treated in Australia and later adopted by Australian families.[48] Those children were some of the earliest members of Australia's Vietnamese community, which today is one of the nation's largest ethnic communities with approximately 300,000 members.[49]

Chapter 3

AERIAL SEARCH AND RESCUE, AERIAL DAMAGE ASSESSMENT AND REPATRIATION OF BODIES VIA AIR

During humanitarian aid and disaster relief (HADR) missions, aerial search and rescue most frequently involves aircrew surveying a disaster zone in search of survivors. The closely related task of aerial damage assessment involves aircrew surveying a disaster zone to assess the extent of damage to infrastructure and natural resources, to minimise deaths and suffering.

Aerial search and rescue

When the Australian Government supports aerial search-and-rescue missions during and following disasters, it most frequently tasks the Australian Defence Force (ADF), which has purpose-designed aircraft with intelligence, surveillance and reconnaissance capabilities. Today, these aircraft include the Boeing E-7A Wedgetail and the Boeing P-8A Poseidon. Before the Poseidon came into ADF service, the Royal Australian Air Force (RAAF) most frequently used the now-retired AP-3C/P-3C Orion for aerial search-and-rescue missions. One memorable Orion mission was the search for the missing German aviator in the South Pacific Ocean in 1997, which featured in the Prologue.

While the RAAF has purpose-designed surveillance aircraft, it is not the only ADF service which conducts aerial search-and-rescue missions. The Royal Australian Navy's (RAN) and Australian Army's helicopters are especially valuable in many search-and-rescue missions, due to their manoeuvrability and, importantly, their ability to fly close to the ground. After Severe Tropical Cyclone *Val* made landfall in Western Samoa in 1991, Army helicopter crews searched for the three missing Australian crewmembers of the fishing boat *Arga J*, which had been wrecked on a reef. Sadly, the crewmembers were never found.[3]

Air Commodore Tony McCormack

Royal Australian Air Force

Tony McCormack (then a wing a commander) with Orion A9-664, the aircraft used in the search-and-rescue mission for the missing German aviator in the South Pacific Ocean in 1997 (Defence)

Search-and-rescue missions are always filled with quiet emotion. No one on a crew will admit it, but you start off nervous, wondering if you will find the survivor. The search phase is full of concentration as you look at every wave and every bit of flotsam or jetsam twice to determine whether it is a survivor or piece of wreckage or not. You hope you have not missed seeing them.[1]

Mission: Missing German aviator in the South Pacific Ocean, 1997

Air Commodore Tony McCormack was involved in the search-and-rescue mission for a German aviator who had ditched his aircraft in the South Pacific Ocean in 1997.

I first became aware Defence was planning a search-and-rescue mission for the missing German aviator while I was in Honiara in the Solomon Islands. I was the executive officer of No 11 Squadron at the time, flying with the crew of AP-3C Orion aircraft A9-664 as a tactical coordinator (TACCO). The aircraft's captain, Lieutenant Smith, an exchange officer from the United States Navy, received a call from No 92 Wing operations back in Australia to advise we would be re-tasked from our routine surveillance patrol in the South Pacific to conduct a search-and-rescue mission for the missing man.

The crew received planning data from the Australian Rescue Coordination Centre through No 92 Wing operations. The information included the last-known position of the survivor, the drift rates for a raft in the open ocean, the weather, and anything that was known about his survival equipment. From this, the crew planned the route to the location, decided on the best search tactics to employ to locate the survivor, determined the nearest airfields to the location for both day and night landings, and calculated how much fuel would be required for each stage of flight.

In addition to our Orion and its crew of around 16 aircrew and maintenance personnel, multiple other people were involved in the search-and-rescue mission, including those at No 92 Wing at RAAF Base Edinburgh in South Australia, the rescue coordination centre in Canberra, along with personnel from Hawaii and the Marshall Islands (with their Pacific patrol boat RMIS *Lomor*).

Using data provided by the Australian search-and-rescue authorities that had factored in the last-known position and drift rates, the crew flew to the predicted position in the ocean. When we were about 30 minutes away, the aircraft descended to the best visual-search altitude and commenced the search. At the same time, as TACCO, I began making calls on the emergency radio frequencies. A short time later, radio contact was made with the survivor and using our onboard electronic systems, the aircraft homed to his position. Visual contact was made with the survivor in his one-person life raft. The raft was so small that visual contact was maintained for less than a second as we flew past.

Knowing maintaining visual contact would be impossible, the crew dropped some sonobuoys around the survivor so we would know he was located inside the circle of sonobuoys. Understandably, the survivor was quite excited that he had been found. But since his rescue by RMIS *Lomor* would still be hours away, we needed to make sure he didn't use up his radio batteries. To do this, a schedule was established where the crew would call him every 30 minutes to check on his welfare and provide him with an update on the arrival time of the patrol boat. In between calls, he was asked to turn his radio off.

In the meantime, RMIS *Lomor* from the Marshall Islands was en route to the survivor's position. Our Orion made contact with the patrol boat to advise them of the latest position of the survivor and to estimate their time of arrival. This was calculated to be about 30 minutes after the time the Orion would have to depart due to fuel limitations. The nearest airfield we could recover to was Nauru, as the closest airfield to the search position, Kiribati, could not be used at night. To conserve fuel, the Orion climbed to 5,000 feet, shut down two of its four engines and commenced an orbit of the survivor's position.

Over the next few hours, as day turned to night, I spoke to the survivor, reassuring him, and continued to direct RMIS *Lomor* to his position. An hour before the patrol boat was due to arrive on the scene, our crew restarted the engines we had shut down to conserve fuel, and descended closer to the water. To help guide the patrol boat to the exact position, we dropped a line of smoke-maker buoys between it and the survivor, and directed the RMIS *Lomor* to follow the line – the survivor would be at the end of it!

As our aircraft commenced its climb and departed for Nauru, I again reassured the survivor, telling him his rescue was only minutes away and that he could contact RMIS *Lomor* on a specific marine radio channel. He wanted to pass some information to us, but we advised him we already had it because, due to the scale of the emergency response, he was the most important person in the Pacific at that time!

As we departed to the west, notification came from the boat that they had rescued the survivor. The crew let out a cheer! Exactly 11.3 hours after we had taken off that morning on our search-and-rescue mission, we landed at Nauru, conducted our post-flight checks on the aircraft, debriefed the sortie and completed the post-flight reports.

We were fortunate during the mission that the weather was good, the aircraft was serviceable and the crew were well trained and professional. Our biggest concerns were to ensure we maintained communication with both the survivor and the patrol boat, that the survivor's radio batteries didn't go flat and that the patrol boat was able to locate him in the dark.

Search-and-rescue missions are always filled with quiet emotion. No one on a crew will admit it, but you start off nervous, wondering if you will find the survivor. The search phase is full of concentration as you look at every wave and every bit of flotsam or jetsam twice to determine whether it is a survivor or piece of wreckage or not. You hope you have not missed seeing them. When a survivor is found, there is a sense of joy that is immediately overtaken by professionalism, as there is still a job to be done. You still need to safely operate the aircraft and get the survivor rescued. Finally, there is an immense sense of pride and satisfaction when the survivor is rescued. On this particular mission, I felt all of these emotions. At the end of the mission, the crew were exhausted but very happy. We later received a thank-you letter from the German Ambassador to Australia.

Search and rescue is not only a national responsibility but it is also our humanitarian duty to assist those in peril. The dedication shown by the crew in the execution of the mission is testament to the importance placed on saving lives. Search and rescue is an important part of what we do in Defence because there are occasions when we are either the nearest to the missing person or disaster location, or we are the only ones who have the capability to respond. In a military sense, it is also important we are able to recover our own personnel who become missing in combat so they don't fall into enemy hands, and if they are injured, so they can receive the best medical care.[2]

Group Captain Roger McCutcheon

Royal Australian Air Force

Group Captain Roger McCutcheon providing a briefing update on the P-8A Poseidon, the successor to the AP-3C Orion (Defence)

We had to consider the safety of our own crew. Due to the extreme range from an airfield, and the sea temperature being about one degree Celsius, our own survival chances were very low if we had an emergency and had to ditch the aircraft into the sea, despite having our own survival equipment on board.[5]

Mission: 1996–97 Vendée Globe around-the-world yacht race

Group Captain Roger McCutcheon was involved in the search-and-rescue effort for British yachtsman Tony Bullimore and French yachtsman Thierry Dubois during the 1996–97 Vendée Globe around-the-world yacht race.

I was a tactical coordinator (TACCO) for No 11 Squadron, on leave in Adelaide in South Australia in early January 1997. I initially heard about the search-and-rescue operation for the two missing yachtsmen through the media on 5 or 6 January, and I called No 92 Wing Operations at RAAF Base Edinburgh in Adelaide to see if they needed any assistance. I was immediately placed on standby and then activated, because many people were not in location due to being on Christmas leave. I didn't have much notice to get to base and deploy: less than 24 hours.

I was TACCO of *Rescue 253* crew, the third P-3C Orion aircraft to deploy. Our initial planning was focused on gathering as much information as possible on the two missing yachtsmen: their last locations and beacon details, both yachts' descriptions and photos, the predicted weather both in the search area and en route, how much time we would have in the search area due to the distance and fuel required, and so on. For me as the crew TACCO, my planning also involved determining which search tactics to employ, such as search patterns, altitude, best search sensors and communication plans, so I could direct the crew in the execution of the search. Other priorities at RAAF Base Edinburgh were getting the aircraft pre-flighted, loading sufficient search-and-rescue stores (such as air–sea rescue kits, sonobuoys, deployable smoke flares and beacons), and then departing as quickly as possible. Planning continued en route to Perth in Western Australia, where we refuelled and then flew to the on-station area located around 3.5-hours southwest of Perth.

Four P-3C Orion aircraft were involved in the mission, with six crews from Nos 10 and 11 Squadrons, plus maintenance and operations support personnel, RAAF Air Command operating from RAAF Base Glenbrook in New South Wales, and RAAF transport aircraft. The RAAF was joined by the RAN's HMAS *Adelaide* and a Seahawk helicopter detachment, along with the Australian Maritime Safety Authority (coordinating the overall search-and-rescue operation), a support oiler ship (HMAS *Westralia*) and a civilian merchant ship (MV *Sanko Phoenix*), which diverted significantly from its course to assist in the effort.

Each Orion crew was a mixture of available personnel from both squadrons: pilots, officer mission aircrew and airborne electronic analysts. Media passengers were also taken on some of the later flights as there was significant national and international media interest in the search-and-rescue effort. Inflight rations were important for such a long and demanding mission, with popular items including chocolate, coffee (instant!) and frozen meals.

The Orion's search-and-rescue sorties were long: around 11 hours airborne, which was near the maximum for an Orion conducting a low-level search. This timeframe allowed about three to 3.5 hours in the search area, with a three- or four-hour transit each way from Perth Airport. We searched mostly at around 300–500 feet altitude, to give us the best chance of visually detecting life rafts or survivors. This altitude was quite turbulent and fatiguing given the wind conditions and sea state. The search area was in the deep Southern Ocean, where none of us had operated before, at around 58th–60th parallel south latitude, not far north of Antarctica. This area is subject to extreme weather conditions, even in summer in early January, with powerful cold fronts rolling through every 12 to 15 hours, resulting in very high winds, rain and snow and very large sea conditions. CSIRO research indicates these seas are some of the worst in the world for weather. Fortunately for my two sorties, we flew between cold fronts, but we could see on the radar the severe weather coming, and the wind and sea states were still large. An interesting planning consideration was whether icebergs would be in the area and how we would detect these at low level! We had to consider the safety of our own crew. Due to the extreme range from an airfield, and the sea temperature being about one degree Celsius, our own survival chances were very low if we had an emergency and had to ditch the aircraft into the sea, despite having our own survival equipment on board.

The last-known positions of the yachtsmen were about 60 nautical miles apart. For Bullimore, his upturned yacht was located visually by the second Orion crew, who were greatly assisted by a satellite datum from his emergency beacon. His actual location was not known, and the search was based on the assumption he had made it into a life raft and been blown downwind. Dubois was located by the first crew on his badly damaged yacht, and several air–sea rescue kits (life rafts and emergency supplies) were dropped to him, which saved his life after his yacht later sank. When my crew arrived on the third sortie, Dubois was in a life raft and we dropped a radio and more supplies to him while also searching for Bullimore. A highlight of the mission was successfully dropping the radio to Dubois and then our crew telling him rescue was on the way and that our aircraft would stay with him as best as we could until then – he was very pleased to hear us!

HMAS *Adelaide* departed from the RAN base HMAS *Stirling* in Western Australia but took three days or so to arrive at the search location, due to the extreme distance. During those three days, our Orion crews continued to relocate Bullimore's yacht, listening on sonobuoys for any signs of life from under the yacht, and searching downwind for his life raft. We also relocated Dubois in his life raft and kept him alive with supplies until HMAS *Adelaide* could arrive.

The search-and-rescue effort lasted for about four or five days until both missing yachtsmen were located and rescued by HMAS *Adelaide*. Two men being rescued in those conditions was excellent. There was suspicion Bullimore may be under his upturned yacht because of some sounds heard via sonobuoys dropped nearby, but we were still quite surprised when he popped up after the RAN crew knocked on the hull! My crew was back in Perth having breakfast after a mission and we saw the rescue imagery on TV. I will never forget that moment when hearing Bullimore was sighted and rescued.

A Canadian yachtsman, Gerry Roufs, later lost his life during the same yacht race in the deep Pacific Ocean, out of the reach of all search-and-rescue capabilities. Bullimore and Dubois were lucky they had been within Australia's search-and-rescue reach, albeit just!

As Australians, we will do everything we can to help people who are in serious trouble in our region. When only the military can help – as was the case for this mission, as no civilian search aircraft had the range – we should absolutely help if we have the capacity.[6]

Air Commodore Craig Heap

Royal Australian Air Force

Craig Heap (then a group captain) talking to Minister Itsunori Onodera, the Japanese Minister of Defense, at RAAF Base Pearce during Operation *Southern Indian Ocean* in 2014 (Defence)

Our dedication to Operation Southern Indian Ocean had been driven by our mutual desire to solve the mystery for the families and loved ones of all who had been on board MH370. It was for them that we searched. We had a noble cause, and a tremendous drive to solve the mystery of what had happened when the aircraft went missing on 8 March 2014.[8]

Mission: Operation *Southern Indian Ocean*, 2014

Air Commodore Craig Heap was involved in Operation Southern Indian Ocean *in 2014, the multi-national HADR mission in search of the missing Malaysian airliner MH370.*

During Operation *Southern Indian Ocean*, I commanded the multinational air task group. This included RAAF Bases Pearce and Learmonth in Western Australia, as well as planning and coordinating the international air-search contributions from the United States, New Zealand, China, Japan, Malaysia and the Republic of Korea. The air task group assembled a coalition of the best maritime aviators in the Pacific, bonded in a common cause to locate the missing MH370 airliner, to conduct what became a search-and-recovery operation.

The Australian Maritime Search Authority (AMSA), which was in charge of the overall search operation, decided where the search would be focused. They based this on guidance from specialist analysts, informed by the AMSA-provided Iridium Self Locating Data Marking Buoy, which AMSA provided to the RAAF and which we deployed from our C-130 Hercules and AP-3C Orion aircraft. The buoy would emit a signal for at least 30 days, broadcasting its global positioning system location back to AMSA. From this information, they could measure and assess its drift over time. AMSA would use this drift model to define the search areas, which they would then allocate to the different nations which were involved. Additionally, specialist acoustic-detection sonobuoys were used to search for the aircraft's cockpit and flight data recorders, which emitted a signal once activated by a significant event (such as a ditching into the ocean) for a period of at least 30 days.

Once all the nations got into the rhythm of the tasking, the operation worked extremely well, despite the challenges of distance, weather and, in some cases, language. Another challenge was that the airliner was predominantly white, and the ocean generally had a lot of white caps. We may have had our defined search areas, but relying on human sight was nonetheless greatly limiting in those conditions.

At one point, we were conducting 10 searches a day, with up to eight aircraft on task at the same time. Low cloud, poor visibility, communication and language difficulties were constant threats, with our key task to synchronise and provide risk controls to minimise the potential for a mid-air collision in the search area. Deconfliction of aircraft by time and search area were key controls in planning every day, which was further complicated by the varying capabilities of the crews and aircraft. A further risk to safe search operations was the potential for helicopters deployed from the surface-search ships to turn up without warning in the same airspace as the fixed-wing aircraft. This made safety my primary concern during Operation *Southern Indian Ocean*: we didn't want another tragedy, especially one of our own making.

To help mitigate the risk of a mid-air collision, we used the RAN's HMAS *Toowoomba*, which has good air-search radar and aircraft-control capability, and two RAAF E-7A Wedgetails. They helped all of the different nations' aircraft by coordinating ingress and egress from the search zone, as well as providing an overwatch and deconfliction advisory service when we were on task.

Operation *Southern Indian Ocean* was, to date, the longest-range maritime air-search operation in history. The search areas ranged from 800 to 1,500 nautical miles from land. At its peak, there were 776 personnel within the Operation *Southern Indian Ocean* air task group. They were from seven nations, they operated up to 20 aircraft and they conducted 339 missions, which included more than 3,000 flying hours. The operation based at RAAF Base Pearce lasted for 42 days and searched an area equivalent to the size of Western Australia. While 185 objects were located, including 70 or so that were photographed, unfortunately none were validated as having come from MH370.

Our dedication to Operation *Southern Indian Ocean* had been driven by our mutual desire to solve the mystery for the families and loved ones of all who had been on board MH370. It was for them that we searched. We had a noble cause and a tremendous drive to solve the mystery of what had happened when the aircraft went missing on 8 March 2014.

We all know in our hearts that we did the best that we possibly could. If *we* couldn't find MH370, no one could. I hope that the shared experiences with our Asian neighbours and other nations during Operation *Southern Indian Ocean* will endure as an example of what we can achieve when we cooperate, united in the one cause.[9]

Flight Lieutenant Cale Barnes

Royal Australian Air Force

Flight Lieutenant Cale Barnes co-pilots a RAAF E-7A Wedgetail deployed in the search for MH370 in 2014 (Defence)

We sent two Wedgetail aircraft to allow us to cover the entire daylight window of the search area. Everyone was excited and keen to go and help in whatever way we could.[10]

Mission: Operation *Southern Indian Ocean*, 2014

Flight Lieutenant Cale Barnes co-piloted a RAAF E-7A Wedgetail during Operation Southern Indian Ocean*, the joint HADR mission in search of missing airliner MH370.*

I was a co-pilot at No 2 Squadron at the time and the missing aircraft was obviously big news. My squadron – which operated the E-7A Wedgetail (an early warning and control aircraft) – wasn't expecting to be involved as the P-3 Orion (a maritime surveillance aircraft) seemed like the more obvious aircraft to assist from a Defence point of view. However, the search grew rapidly in the number of assets involved and that is when there was a request to send the Wedgetail to assist with the search and to provide a communications relay.

Our planning for the mission included considerations of the maximum distance offshore to which we could travel (to be within the confines of restrictions related to a single engine failure), and also the best altitude to hold at to maximise our time on station, due to no air-to-air refuelling being available.

There were three or four crews (with approximately 10 people per crew) sent over to Western Australia to begin with, with a day or two's notice. We had no end date when we were first tasked and we didn't know where we would be operating from. We sent two Wedgetail aircraft to allow us to cover the entire daylight window of the search area. Everyone was excited and keen to go and help in whatever way we could.

We started out operating out of Perth Airport for about a week, before the search area moved north and we relocated to RAAF Base Learmonth near Exmouth in Western Australia.[11] The sorties when searching for MH370 were generally about eight or nine hours long and involved transiting approximately 1,000 nautical miles (1,852 kilometres) offshore to the search area. We would descend from our transit altitude of around 30,000 feet to hold at approximately 24,000 feet, for maximum endurance on station. We would be on station for about five hours, depending on holding requirements due to the weather back at RAAF Base Learmonth. Between the two aircraft we took, we could generally cover the entire daytime search window with a small crossover period when the second jet would come out to relieve the first.

One challenge we experienced was during a period of a week or so when several severe storms came through and cut off RAAF Base Learmonth. We were still able to conduct our missions, but the base was starting to run low of general everyday supplies.

We were deployed for approximately a month overall before our portion was wrapped up and the focus of the search was primarily being run with ships.

This was my first 'real' deployment in which I was actually supplying a service in support of something that wasn't an exercise or for training. So, it was great to be involved with something so important and to provide assistance where I could. While HADR is not my squadron's primary mission, when we have the capability to provide it, we should, as it goes a long way to developing positive relationships.[12]

During the 1996–97 Vendée Globe around-the-world single-handed yacht race, British yachtsman Tony Bullimore and French yachtsman Thierry Dubois both went missing – at the same time but 60 nautical miles apart – in the deep Southern Ocean just north of Antarctica. The extensive search-and-rescue effort that followed included RAAF Orion aircraft and RAN S-70B Seahawk helicopters, before both men were rescued by the crew of the RAN's HMAS *Adelaide*. More recently, during Operation *Flood Assist* in 2022 – in which heavy rainfall led to widespread flooding throughout much of Australia – RAN and Army aircrews used their MH-60R Seahawk and MRH-90 Taipan helicopters to rescue 113 people stranded on the roofs of buildings and cars.[4]

Search-and-rescue missions are often joint activities involving several nations. One reason for this is that these missions are frequently conducted to search for survivors of aviation disasters, which typically have passengers from many nations on board. A well-known example is the disappearance in mysterious circumstances of Malaysia Airlines Flight 370 (MH370) in 2014. The Boeing 777 was en route from Kuala Lumpur in Malaysia to Beijing in China when it vanished from radar with 239 passengers and crewmembers on board. Operation *Southern Indian Ocean* was the large-scale search-and-rescue mission led by the Australian Maritime Safety Authority (AMSA) and involving many nations. All three ADF services deployed multiple aircraft, including four Orions and two Wedgetails operating out of RAAF Bases Pearce and Learmonth in Western Australia.[7] Despite an extensive search of more than 2,000 square kilometres of ocean, no passengers or crew, either dead or alive, have been found to date.

A RAAF C-17 returning to Eindhoven Airfield in the Netherlands following a search-and-rescue sortie to Ukraine during Operation *Bring Them Home* in 2014 (Defence)

Later that year, Malaysia Airlines Flight 17, a scheduled flight from Amsterdam in the Netherlands to Kuala Lumpur in Malaysia, crashed in Ukraine after being hit by a Russian missile. During Operation *Bring Them Home*, the RAAF conducted 10 aerial search-and-rescue sorties over 32 square kilometres in Ukraine, but none of the 283 passengers and 15 crewmembers had survived.[13] Also in 2014, Indonesia AirAsia Flight 8501, a scheduled flight from Surabaya in Indonesia to Singapore, crashed into the Java Sea. The RAAF deployed AP-3C Orions as part of the international search-and-rescue effort, but none of the 162 people on board were found alive.[14]

Aerial damage assessment

The Australian Government most frequently tasks the ADF – with its purpose-designed intelligence, surveillance and reconnaissance aircraft – to conduct aerial damage assessment following a disaster. This role has an HADR effect when the damage assessment is then used to minimise deaths and suffering. For example, the assessment that a body of water used by a community for drinking and hygiene has been contaminated by a disaster (such as volcanic ash) can prompt the HADR effort to prioritise the distribution of safe drinking water before anyone becomes ill.

The RAAF deployed Orion aircraft to assess damage during missions including Operation *Aspen* following Cyclone *Betsy* in Vanuatu in 1992, Operation *Yasi Assist* following Severe Tropical Cyclone *Yasi* in northern Queensland in 2011, and Operation *Pacific Assist 2015* following Severe Tropical Cyclone *Pam* in Vanuatu and the Solomon Islands.[15] The Orion's replacement, the P-8 Poseidon, has deployed for damage assessment during missions including Operation *Fiji Assist 2020* following Cyclone *Yasa*, Operation *Bushfire Assist* in Australia in 2020, Operation *Flood Assist* in Australia in 2022, and Operation *Tonga Assist 2022* following the eruption of the Hunga Tonga–Hunga Ha'apai volcano.[16]

However, since the earliest days of aerial damage-assessment missions, the ADF has also used aircraft not specifically designed for the role, but which have been modified for the purpose. After Mount Lamington erupted in New Guinea in 1951, the RAAF used modified de Havilland DH.98 Mosquitos to photograph the volcano and the damage it had caused, flying within 60 metres of the still-smoking crater.[17] More recently, during Operation *Tonga Assist 2022*, the RAAF flew a modified C-130J Hercules, fitted with live-stream capability, over Tonga to record the damage and to allow assessment teams to plan the following HADR effort to best minimise suffering.[18] Commanding Officer No 37 Squadron, Wing Commander Anthony Kay, observed: 'Our Hercules crews have generations of experience in delivering disaster assistance across the region, but this capability is yielding new ways to support the Pacific Island community.'[19]

Repatriation of bodies via air

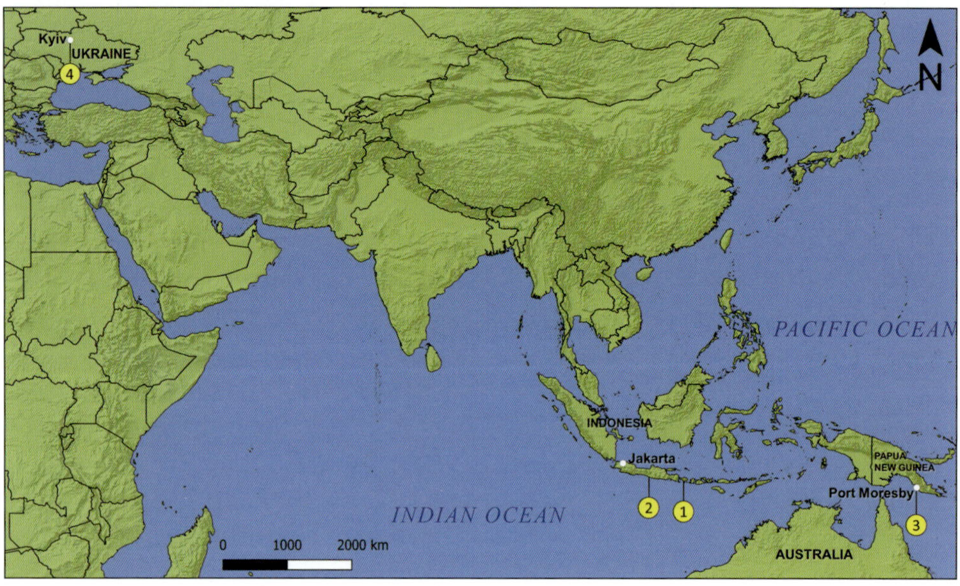

Selected Australian Defence Force aerial repatriation missions: global

1. Operation *Bali Assist*, Indonesia, 2002
2. Garuda Indonesia Flight 200, Indonesia, 2007
3. Operation *Kokoda Assist*, Papua New Guinea, 2009
4. Operation *Bring Them Home*, Ukraine, 2014

RAAF personnel preparing to move caskets onto a C-130J Hercules at Port Moresby International Airport in Papua New Guinea during Operation *Kokoda Assist* in 2009 (Defence)

When the Australian Government seeks to bring home the bodies of Australian citizens who have lost their lives in disasters overseas, it most frequently tasks the ADF with this sad duty. Perhaps in reflection of our globetrotting culture, a high proportion of these Australians have historically been the victims of aviation accidents. Garuda Indonesia Flight 200, a scheduled passenger flight from Jakarta to Yogyakarta, both in Indonesia, crashed into a rice field upon landing in 2007, killing 21 people. The RAAF repatriated to Canberra the bodies of the five Australians who had been killed.[20] In a similar incident close to the hearts of many Australians – for whom the Kokoda Track holds strong symbolic value – Airlines PNG Flight 4684 crashed near Kokoda in Papua New Guinea in 2009, killing all 13 passengers and crewmembers. During Operation *Kokoda Assist*, the RAAF repatriated the bodies of the nine Australians who had been on board.[21]

One of the ADF's most memorable repatriation missions followed the crash of MH17, which had been hit by a Russian missile over Ukraine in 2014. During Operation *Bring Them Home*, two RAAF C-17 Globemasters and their crews were central to the mission to recover, identify and repatriate the bodies of the 37 Australians who had been on board.[22] One of the loadmasters during the repatriation mission, Warrant Officer Wayne Silverman, reflected:

> Putting the caskets on [the aircraft], you're just putting them on, tying them down, you're not thinking about who those people are. But when it cuts you in half is when the relatives come on [board]. They thank you, they hug you, they show you pictures of their family and they talk about the people they've lost.[23]

A C-17, carrying the remains of victims of the MH17 crash, preparing to leave Ukraine for the Netherlands during Operation *Bring Them Home* in 2014 (Defence)

National flags fly at half-mast as hearses carrying the remains of victims of the MH17 crash leave Eindhoven Airfield in the Netherlands. In the background, a RAAF C-17 is preparing to repatriate the bodies of the Australians as part of Operation *Bring Them Home* (Defence)

The 2002 Bali bombings in Indonesia – in which 202 people lost their lives – was a rare occasion when both military and commercial aircraft repatriated the bodies of Australians. In this case, the Department of Foreign Affairs and Trade tasked both the ADF and Qantas to repatriate the 88 Australians who had lost their lives in the terrorist attack.[24]

Chapter 4

TRANSPORTING PERSONNEL TO PROVIDE HUMANITARIAN AID AND DISASTER RELIEF

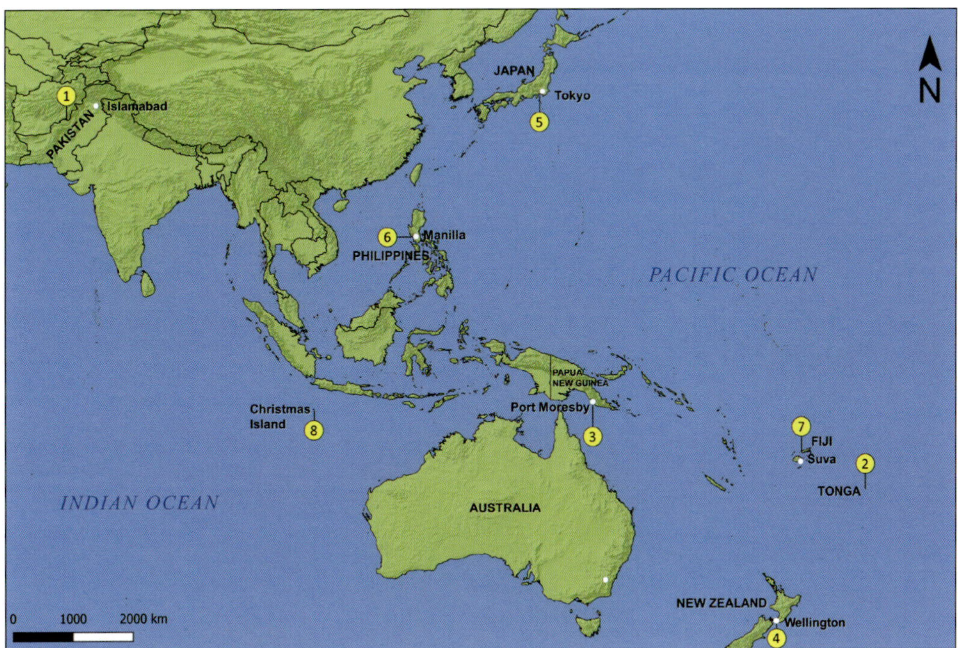

Selected Australian Defence Force missions to transport personnel to provide humanitarian aid and disaster relief: Asia–Pacific

1. Operation *Pakistan Assist I*, 2005–6 & Operation *Longreach*, Pakistan, 2006
2. Operation *Ashika Assist*, Tonga, 2009
3. Operation *Kokoda Assist*, Papua New Guinea, 2009 & Operation *Kimba*, Papua New Guinea, 2022
4. Operation *Christchurch Assist*, New Zealand, 2011
5. Operation *Pacific Assist 2011*, Japan
6. Operation *Philippines Assist*, 2013
7. Operation *Fiji Assist 2016*
8. Quarantine of Australians from Wuhan in China, Christmas Island, 2020

The many and various needs of a nation following a disaster require specialised skills to help meet those needs. The use of Australian air power in humanitarian aid and disaster relief (HADR) efforts therefore often includes transporting personnel with specific skillsets to the sites of disasters. When tasked by the Australian Government, both the Australian Defence Force (ADF) and commercial airlines have historically transported these personnel.

Selected Australian Defence Force missions to transport personnel to provide humanitarian aid and disaster relief: Europe/Africa

1. Operation *Bring Them Home*, Ukraine, 2014
2. Operation *Aslan*, South Sudan, 2013

I. The Australian Defence Force transporting personnel

Medical personnel

After a disaster leaves many people injured – such as a terrorist attack or significant natural disaster – the ADF will work hard to transport medical personnel to the disaster site as quickly as possible so they can start their lifesaving work. During Operation *Sumatra Assist I* in 2004, within 36 hours of the Boxing Day tsunami, the Royal Australian Air Force (RAAF) transported two medical teams funded by Australian Aid to Indonesia on four C-130 Hercules aircraft.[1] The ADF responded similarly quickly after Typhoon *Haiyan/Yolanda* struck the Philippines in 2013, leaving 7,360 people dead or missing, injuring 27,000 people and displacing more than four million.[2] During Operation *Philippines Assist,* the RAAF rapidly transported a medical team to establish a 50-bed field hospital, along with 25 tonnes of emergency supplies.[3] The head of the 36-member medical team from the National Critical Care and Trauma Response Centre, Dr Ian Norton, observed: 'We are going into a region that is still just reeling and recovering. So the response pace is very, very active.'[4]

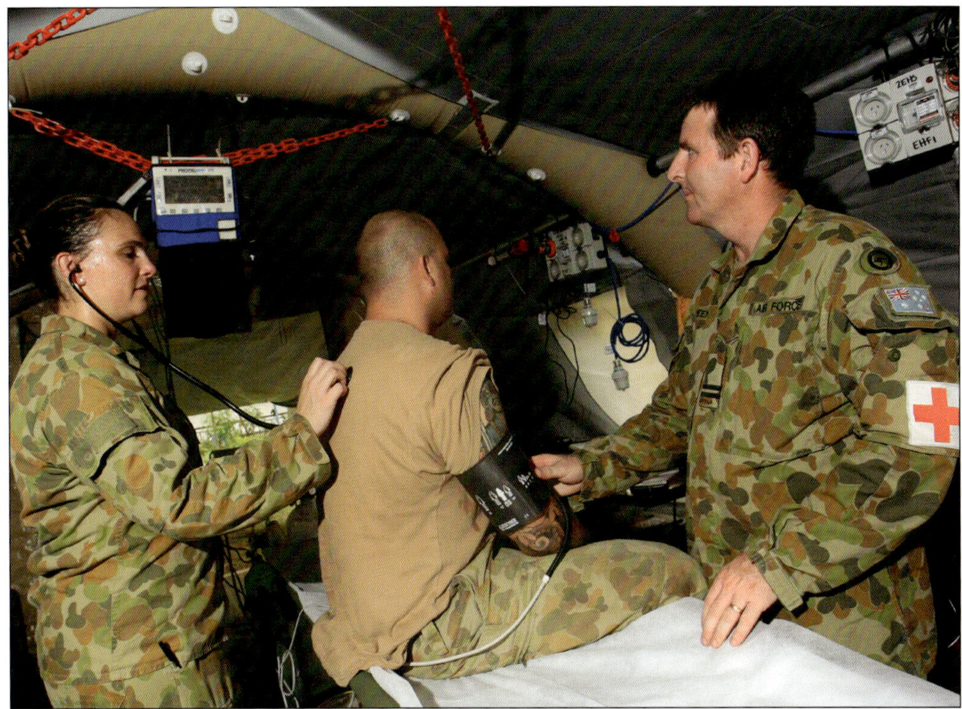

RAAF medical officer Flight Lieutenant Danielle Jolly and nurse Flight Lieutenant Paul Green examining a patient during Operation *Philippines Assist* in 2013 (Defence)

Operation *COVID-19 Assist* (2020–22) presented the ADF with many opportunities to transport medical personnel to provide HADR. The RAAF transported medical personnel and critical medical equipment to Fiji on two separate missions. These medical teams worked alongside Fiji's frontline health workers at community healthcare facilities to help control

Squadron Leader Cameron Brockel

Royal Australian Air Force

Squadron Leader Cameron Brockel (foreground) with Bronte Martin, AUSMAT Specialist Coordination Team lead, outside the North West Regional Hospital in Burnie in Tasmania in 2020 during Operation *COVID-19 Assist* (Defence)

Engaging in HADR shows that Australia and Australians are concerned for the welfare and wellbeing of others in times of crisis. Helping out on HADR missions is why I joined the Air Force.[8]

Mission: Operation *COVID-19 Assist*, 2020

Squadron Leader Cameron Brockel was the officer in charge of the ADF's medical team during a combined ADF/AUSMAT mission to resume emergency medical services at the North West Regional Hospital in Tasmania, after the hospital had closed following an outbreak of COVID-19.

I first became aware of this task when I received a phone call early on Easter Saturday, 11 April 2020, asking me to determine personnel availability for 'a task that was on the news'. I had not yet seen the story and was completely unaware up until that point.

This was a very short-notice tasking. The RAAF's Headquarters Health Services Wing and Headquarters Joint Operations Command conducted all of the initial health planning. As the officer in charge of the clinical flight, I was initially involved in allocating team members from No 1 Expeditionary Health Service to the task. Then, late on Easter Saturday, I was tasked as the mission lead.

On 14 April 2020, two C-130 Hercules aircraft deployed from RAAF Amberley in Queensland and RAAF Bases Richmond and Williamtown in New South Wales with the majority of the ADF and some AUSMAT personnel, to Burnie Airport in Tasmania. A contracted Learjet aircraft transported the Darwin-based AUSMAT personnel and then, a few days into the mission, another contracted Learjet transported additional personnel to Tasmania.

The 52 members from the RAN, Army and RAAF were a diverse team of emergency department physicians, general practitioners, nurses, environmental health officers, medical officers, scientific officers, radiographers, pharmacists, public affairs officers, medical technicians, personnel capability specialists, dental assistants and drivers. The seven AUSMAT personnel included an emergency department physician, nurses (including two emergency-department nurses and an infection-control nurse), a logistics specialist and a paramedic.

Our joint mission was to re-establish the civilian emergency department at North West Regional Hospital and to maintain critical medical services to the local community. As the ADF commander for the mission, I worked with the AUSMAT team lead to develop systems to operate the emergency department in the midst of the COVID-19 pandemic. This was pre-vaccine when there were many unknowns, and the risk of serious illness or death was high.

Between 14 and 16 April, when the entire emergency department was being terminally cleaned, we conducted tactical planning and training for team members. On 17 April, when we were finally given access to the emergency department, we re-established all of the equipment, conducted training and rehearsals, and then opened to the public by 6pm that day.

We divided the ADF personnel into two clinical teams who worked 12-hour shifts continuously over 12 days in the emergency department, with mentoring and policy support from AUSMAT. The early days were very hard as we were facing many unknowns, in an uncertain situation, with limited clinical expertise, in a high-tempo and high-acuity environment. The lack of understanding of the virus made it challenging.

The ultimate outcome was a highly successful mission: we provided high-quality emergency health services to the north-west Tasmanian community, then handed over to the hospital staff on their return from illness or isolation. We experienced an incredibly positive reaction and plenty of gratitude from the community: the patients whom we treated provided overwhelmingly positive feedback. When the Tasmanian health personnel returned to take over again, they were also grateful for all that we had done. The ADF and AUSMAT teams departed Burnie on 30 April and we all went into two weeks' quarantine.

A highlight of the mission for me was seeing the rapid development of the team from uncertainty and trepidation to a high level of competence and confidence. This gave me a great deal of respect and admiration for the medical personnel whom I work with and their adaptability, competence and potential.

Engaging in HADR shows that Australia and Australians are concerned for the welfare and wellbeing of others in times of crisis. Helping out on HADR missions is why I joined the Air Force.[9]

the infection. The RAAF also deployed a C-17 to Honiara in the Solomon Islands, with members of the Australian Medical Assistance Team (AUSMAT) and critical medical supplies on board, in response to a surge of COVID-19 cases in the island nation.[5] Back home in Australia, the North West Regional Hospital in Tasmania was forced to close in 2020 following an outbreak of the virus, so the RAAF transported a combined ADF and AUSMAT medical team to resume emergency medical services at the hospital.[6] The officer in charge of the ADF component, Squadron Leader Cameron Brockel, reflected:

> What we achieved was unprecedented. We started with a bare hospital, one that none of our team had ever seen before, and had set up an operational emergency department within six hours.[7]

Cameraman Greg Barbera (centre) from the Australian television program *60 Minutes* filming a medical team unloading equipment from an Australian Army Black Hawk helicopter in a mountain village in Pakistan. The ADF deployed on Operation *Longreach* following the devastating Kashmir earthquake in 2005 (Defence)

Villagers waiting outside the ADF's temporary health centre in Bailgiran village in the mountains of Pakistan during Operation *Longreach* (Defence)

Often after a disaster has occurred, the need for medical care is great in remote and difficult-to-reach locations. This was the case following the devastating Kashmir earthquake in Pakistan in 2005 which killed at least 86,000 people and injured at least 69,000 more. Through Operation *Longreach*, the Army transported medical teams via Black Hawk helicopters to a remote village in Pakistan, where they set up and operated a temporary health centre.[10] The teams provided 900 medical treatments and 1,500 vaccinations to the villagers to help prevent further deaths.[11] The operational name 'Longreach' (a town in outback Queensland) was well chosen due to the remoteness of the Pakistani villages that needed support.

Search-and-rescue personnel

The Australian Government frequently tasks the ADF to transport search-and-rescue workers to disaster sites to attempt to locate and rescue missing people and thereby minimise the number of lives lost. When the disaster has occurred in a densely populated area, the assistance of urban search-and-rescue (USAR) workers can be invaluable. This was the case after a 6.2-magnitude earthquake struck Christchurch in New Zealand in 2011, killing 185 people.[12] During Operation *Christchurch Assist*, the RAAF transported 148 civilian USAR workers to help locate and rescue survivors who were trapped underneath rubble.[13] Former attorney-general of Australia Robert McClelland observed: 'These rescue teams are experts at recovering people who are trapped or affected by structural collapse. They have expert search, rescue, medical, engineering and support capabilities.'[14]

Personnel from Queensland Urban Search and Rescue Task Force 1 on board a RAAF C-17 prior to departing for New Zealand. The ADF transported the workers to search for survivors of the 2011 Christchurch earthquake (Defence)

More recently, a RAAF C-17 Globemaster transported 72 civilian USAR personnel to Türkiye after a series of devastating earthquakes struck the nation in early 2023.[15] As the death toll continued to rise in the days following the earthquakes, the need escalated for specialists to help locate people still trapped beneath rubble. The chief superintendent of the AUS 2 Disaster Assistance Response Team, Darryl Dunbar, stated prior to arriving in Türkiye:

> We're unsure what we will find at first but will do our best to support the people of Türkiye in their hour of need. We find solutions to any challenges we face. That's what we train for and our team are prepared.[16]

USAR teams often include search-and-rescue dogs, who are trained in airborne-scent detection and trailing which makes them effective in USAR missions: using their noses, they can locate people who may not be able to call or signal for help. During Operation *Pacific Assist 2011* following the Tōhoku earthquake, tsunami and Fukushima Daiichi Nuclear Power Plant meltdown, the RAAF transported a USAR team which included two search-and-rescue dogs and their handlers.[17] Air Commodore Tony McCormack, who was posted to the Yokota Air Base and experienced the disaster firsthand, observed the dogs were 'the most famous dogs in Japan at the time. They were covered everywhere in the media.'[18]

Depending on the circumstances of the disaster, search-and-rescue workers sometimes expect to find only bodies, not survivors. Yet sometimes they cannot even locate bodies. And at other times, they may know where bodies are but be unable to recover them. This was the case during Operation *Ashika Assist*, after an estimated 85 people, all women and children, drowned when the civilian ferry *Princess Ashika* sank in Tonga in 2009.[19] In response to a call for assistance from the Government of Tonga, the RAAF transported a team of 16 Royal Australian Navy (RAN) divers to assist with locating the sunken ferry and bringing bodies back to the surface.[20] Sadly, because the ferry had sunk in extremely deep water, no bodies could be recovered.[21]

Left to right: Chris Purcill, Frayer, Tilda and Barry Lowday from Queensland Search and Rescue preparing to depart for Japan via a RAAF C-17 during Operation *Pacific Assist 2011* (Defence)

Petty Officer Scott Broughton

Royal Australian Navy

Able Seaman Chris Bowler assisting Scott Broughton (then a seaman, seated) during diving drills at His Majesty's Navy Base Masefield in Tonga during Operation *Ashika Assist* in 2009 (Defence)

Small countries such as Tonga are not always equipped to deal with these types of situations. Engaging in HADR therefore helps us to establish relationships, trust and confidence in each other as neighbouring countries. Helping one another in times of need is paramount.[22]

Mission: Operation *Ashika Assist*, 2009

Petty Officer Scott Broughton was part of a team of 16 RAN divers who were tasked to search for bodies after the ferry Princess Ashika *sank in Tonga in 2009 with 141 people on board.*

On the morning of Friday 7 August 2009, I arrived at work – Clearance Diving TEAM 1 at HMAS *Waterhen* in New South Wales – at 7:30 am, as I did on any other working day. At 7:45 am, we all came together to conduct what's called 'both watches' to discuss what the day would entail. Being a Friday, I was expecting to do a normal maintenance day to close out the working week. It was during both watches we were told an incident had occurred in Tonga and that a handful of divers would be deploying to assist with the recovery effort. The names of those who were to deploy were read out: mine was one of them. In the briefing room, we were brought up to speed with what had happened and what we were going to do. We were given an hour to head home, pack what we needed, and return ready to depart for RAAF Base Richmond, where our two C-130 Hercules aircraft would be waiting. Those who weren't deploying prepared the equipment required for the operation.

I was quite junior at that point in time: I held the rank of seaman and was fresh from graduating from my basic clearance diving course. I was probably the newest one in the team chosen to deploy. Upon my return to HMAS *Waterhen* after packing, I loaded the decompression chamber and air cylinders onto a truck ready for transport out to RAAF Base Richmond, where we were met by the RAAF air load team. Our equipment was loaded onto a separate C-130 Hercules to the divers and flown over to Tonga separately. This equipment included a recompression chamber, standard scuba dive equipment, surface supplied breathing apparatus, Zodiac inflatable boats and their engines.

The flight was uneventful and took about five hours; we had ration packs with sandwiches, fruit and bottled water en route. After we arrived in Tonga, we unpacked our equipment and completed dive drills with surface-supplied breathing apparatus inside the boat harbour in Nuku'alofa. At this time, the Tongan authorities were still trying to exactly locate the ferry.

We had been told all of the men on board had escaped and the thought of having to recover women and children from the wreck was especially challenging. It really sank in what we were there to do when the vessel's location was identified and a large number of body bags were loaded onto the Tonga Royal Navy vessel, which would take us out to the location of the sinking.

It took us around four to five hours to get to the site; we arrived about an hour before sunset. I was chosen to do the first dive – as it turned out, my dive was the only dive of the mission! We launched the Zodiac using the vessel's crane; due to the conditions on the day, it was tough getting it into the water and then safely passing down all of the dive equipment we needed.

We had been told prior to the dive that the *Princess Ashika*'s bowline (rope) had been seen floating just below the surface. It was hoped the ship was still attached to the other end. We pushed away from the Tongan vessel in the Zodiac to try to locate the rope. A short time later, we found a thick natural fibre hawser (a rope used to tie a ship) sitting just on the surface. I got into my diving gear and jumped into the water. I remember seeing another Tongan vessel whose crew was using a pool scoop with a long pole to recover what looked like body parts and belongings from the water.

I left the surface and began the dive; the sun was setting and visibility subsurface was not the best. The water was a deep, dark blue, consistent with open-water deep dives. As I got close to my maximum depth of 50 metres, I could see a silhouette consistent with the size and shape of the *Princess Ashika*, but nothing to confirm it was the same ship. I tried to look for something that could be used as a key identifying feature. But the light was poor and fading quickly; unfortunately, all I could see was a ship of the right size and shape sitting at a depth of around 100 metres.

Back on the surface, it was getting dark, and dangerous with the sea swell. I was recovered back into the Zodiac and we returned to the navy vessel, where I debriefed my chain of command on what I had seen.

The next day, the Royal New Zealand Navy used their remotely operated underwater vehicle to assess the site. They confirmed the ship was in fact the *Princess Ashika* and that it was sitting at 100 metres or deeper. Unfortunately, due to the depth of the water, no bodies could be recovered.

Before we left Tonga, we were invited to a local church for a service for those who had been lost during the sinking of the ferry. The church was a big white timber building: a place of worship, song and dance. The locals were very thankful for what we had done. This was a highlight for me of the mission: seeing how the Tongans live and experiencing their culture. We were later invited to the governor-general's house for lunch, as well as a number of other local dinners, before meeting the RAAF aircraft for our return flight to Australia.

Small countries such as Tonga are not always equipped to deal with these types of situations. Engaging in HADR therefore helps us to establish relationships, trust and confidence in each other as neighbouring countries. Helping one another in times of need is paramount. It also gives us the opportunity to do what we are trained to do.[23]

Disaster-mitigation personnel

The nature of some disasters – such as wars or bushfires – means their severity, including their cost on human lives, may be reduced with timely human intervention. In such cases, the ADF may transport Defence or civilian personnel to help combat the disaster while it is still unfolding. Prior to the COVID-19 era, the best-known example of this was the transportation of firefighters. As recorded in *ADF Air Power*:

> The Australian summer of 2019–20 brought with it one of the most devastating bushfire seasons on record. Affecting over 46 million acres, 3,500 homes and thousands of people, it represented a major humanitarian crisis that lasted almost nine months.[24]

During Operation *Bushfire Assist*, the RAAF transported civilian firefighters from around Australia to the areas under greatest threat.[25] During this operation, ADF aircraft 'were also used for fire spotting and to increase the perspective of commanders who flew over the affected areas.'[26] In this way, the aircraft themselves were a valuable resource to help mitigate the scale of the disaster.

Firefighters from Fire and Rescue NSW disembarking from a RAAF C-130J Hercules into smoke haze in Canberra during Operation *Bushfire Assist* in 2020 (Defence)

Yet during the COVID-19 pandemic, the deployment of frontline personnel during disasters often translated to people working to contain the virus. During the earliest months of the pandemic – even before Operation *COVID-19 Assist* had been officially stood up as an operation – the ADF was part of a coalition of government agencies working to contain the virus through quarantine. In early 2020, personnel from 14 different ADF units deployed to assist with the quarantine on Christmas Island of Australians who had evacuated from Wuhan in China, the city where the virus had originated.[27] The commander of the joint ADF task unit on Christmas Island, Colonel Phil Baldoni, stated:

> With minimum direction, my team leaders on the ground used their initiative and got things done to meet the needs of evacuees. I'm incredibly proud of the efforts they made to help their fellow Australians.[28]

Colonel Phil Baldoni

Australian Army

Phil Baldoni (then a lieutenant colonel) at the time of the quarantine of Australians on Christmas Island due to the COVID-19 virus (Defence)

Reflecting on HADR, I don't think there is a more tangible way of demonstrating (and not just saying) to vulnerable people, 'I'm from the government and I'm here to help.'[29]

Mission: Quarantine of Australians from Wuhan in China, 2020

During the first months of the COVID-19 pandemic in 2020, Colonel Phil Baldoni helped to support the quarantine on Christmas Island of Australians who had evacuated from Wuhan.

On 30 January 2020, my boss, Commander of 17th Brigade (17BDE), rang me and gave me a verbal warning order that an evacuation from Wuhan was being considered, that the likely quarantine location was Christmas Island, and that he had asked for 17BDE to take the lead on providing the headquarters. Planning developed rapidly.

There was a lot of concurrent activity from units across 17BDE, 6th Brigade, 1st Brigade and others to get prepared. At the time, my battalion – 9th Force Support Battalion – was 17BDE's 'online' force support battalion to provide short-notice elements. From the issue of the warning order to having all elements arrive on Christmas Island (which was the first time I saw all of the task units in one place!) was 44 hours, and we were ready to receive evacuees 22.5 hours after that.

The joint mission would involve several phases, including establishing the quarantine facility at Christmas Island, transferring the Australian evacuees to the island, quarantining the evacuees in line with government requirements, transporting the evacuees to Australia following their quarantine period, and disestablishing the quarantine facility.

Before we deployed, the hard part of the planning effort was trying to get a plan together for how we were going to run what was effectively a low-dependency hospital inside a detention centre thousands of kilometres away, with no sustainment architecture. My operations team submitted air-movement requests to the RAAF's Air Mobility Control Centre, and worked through the 1st Joint Movement Unit using the standard (albeit very accelerated) process for movement planning.

The speed of execution did not allow us to force concentrate in one location, so we had part of the task unit force concentrate in RAAF Amberley in Queensland, and others force concentrate in RAAF Base Darwin in the Northern Territory. With limited time to plan and gather information on what was available for our use on Christmas Island, our initial equipment movement bill was pretty heavy: among other things, we took a Toyota Landcruiser from 9th Force Support Battalion, and a company's worth of stores from 1st Brigade, including tents, generators and so on, in case we needed them.

We deployed on four C-130 Hercules aircraft. The Amberley-origin flights bounced briefly through Darwin and then straight on to Christmas Island. I recall lots of shouted conversations with my operations team as we compared notes, scribbled on maps and finalised the wire diagram/command structure on the way.

Once we got onto the island, we had access to a RAAF C-130 aircraft every couple of days. These were vital. We discovered there were no available vehicles on the island to move 200+ people from the airport to the detention facility, so our first urgent request was for Unimogs [multi-purpose trucks] and some small buses. The Unimogs arrived in time for us to move the evacuees, but the buses never eventuated and to this day I do not know why. We ended up using Toyota HiAces owned by the Australian Border Force (ABF), which had been taken out of service for disposal. These were rapidly inspected by our vehicle maintenance team to ensure they were safe and were subsequently used for people movement.

The RAAF aircraft were vital for the delivery of fresh food. The ADF contingent and evacuees made up about 20% of the population of Christmas Island during our time there, and the island hadn't had a commercial delivery of fresh food for around six weeks. So even if there had been food available locally, we would have rapidly exhausted local supplies.

My team was confined to the detention centre out of respect for community concerns (remembering the disease and its transmission vectors were not well understood at the time). The air load team, who worked out of the airport, were champions: they were absolutely a vital part of the task. They worked all hours to get loads ready for the return to the mainland. In particular, the return of the shippers used to move refrigerated fresh food. There weren't enough of these in the system, so if we didn't get them emptied and loaded onto the next flight back, there would be no more available to move the next load of fresh food (and the supply of fresh food was vital for evacuee welfare and morale). They also worked closely and effectively with the ABF and Department of Agriculture, Fisheries and Forestry personnel to ensure we met the quarantine requirements for equipment returning to the mainland. Their work was an important piece in establishing trust with the other government agencies on the island. That is vital when getting the task done relies on relationships rather than command authority, and in interagency operations such as HADR, that is the norm rather than the exception.

The responses of the evacuees who were being quarantined on Christmas Island varied. Initially, there was a degree of shock: the conditions on the island were not exactly what the evacuees had expected. Also, arriving in the middle of the night in a strange place and being met by uniformed personnel (ADF and ABF) in masks and gloves, and medical personnel in full protective gear, can't have been fun. There was initial unhappiness over the food, but stringent efforts by the Northern Command staff to get the fresh food supply chain up and running, and amazing work by our catering section, turned that around quite quickly. We put a lot of effort into reassuring people they were going to be looked after.

On the day the first contingent of evacuees was due to leave Christmas Island for Australia, we had a communal breakfast to say goodbye. It was the first time we'd been able to interact with evacuees without masks and gloves. That was a pretty good day at the office.

The ultimate outcome was that the Australian Government successfully returned 278 healthy Australians to Australia via Christmas Island. More went through Howard Springs in the Northern Territory later in the task.

Reflecting on HADR, I don't think there is a more tangible way of demonstrating (and not just saying) to vulnerable people, 'I'm from the government and I'm here to help.' When it involves Australians helping Australians through Defence Assistance to the Civil Community tasks, it is the social contract between government and people in action. It's the essence of 'actions speak louder than words'.[30]

Squadron Leader David Weekley

Royal Australian Air Force

Squadron Leader David Weekley (second from left) with the reconnaissance team at Christmas Island Airport prior to receiving Australian evacuees from Wuhan (Paul McFarlane)

Ever since I was a young child, I have heard the media promote the vision of 'the Australian way'. Whenever I play a part in an HADR mission, I am reminded of what that statement means to me: it means getting the job done, no matter the challenges or the difficulties.[31]

Mission: Quarantine of Australians from Wuhan in China, 2020

During the first months of the COVID-19 pandemic in 2020, Squadron Leader David Weekley helped to support the quarantine on Christmas Island of Australians who had evacuated from Wuhan.

I was unaware of the plan for an HADR mission on Christmas Island until I received a phone call from my higher headquarters on 29 January 2020. The discussion centred on the possibility of me flying to Christmas Island to provide airbase subject-matter expertise to a small reconnaissance team. I was at RAAF Base East Sale in Victoria on Operation *Bushfire Assist* at the time, but I was nearing completion and had just booked my travel from Melbourne to my home location in Brisbane in Queensland.

All through my career, whenever I have been asked to deploy to any location, either within Australia or overseas, I have said 'yes'. This time was no exception and I replied that I was excited to assist with this mission. I departed the very next day. At that stage, I had no idea what, if any, planning had taken place and what requests for information I would need to investigate once arriving on Christmas Island.

Until I met with two Army personnel and a member of the Australian Medical Assistance Team (AUSMAT) in Perth in Western Australia about two hours prior to our flight to Christmas Island on 31 January, I still had very little knowledge of the mission or what expertise I was to provide. The Army lieutenant colonel informed us of the potential mission and advised us we would have to begin work as soon as we landed at approximately 7:40 pm. It was at this stage I realised how rapidly the team had been put together, and how vital our reconnaissance team was to enable further planning at Headquarters Joint Operations Command.

The key aim of our tasking was to provide ADF support to the whole-of-government mission to keep the Wuhan evacuees safe and healthy on Christmas Island, and enable their return to Australia without the virus being transported into Australia. The other main outcomes were to ensure the Christmas Island residents were not put at any risk of contracting the virus, and ensuring the infrastructure and flora and fauna on the island were not damaged.

On the flight to Christmas Island, we began reviewing the requests for information in detail. We were still unaware of the specifics required to begin detailed planning, such as what support and infrastructure were already available on the island, when support aircraft would begin arriving from Australia, and when evacuees would begin arriving from Wuhan in China, let alone how many.

On arrival on Christmas Island, I met with the civilian airport manager and we discussed the impending arrival of up to three C-130J Hercules aircraft and a C-17A Globemaster, which were bringing support equipment and personnel to assist with preparing the airport, ground transport, accommodation and rations for the arrival, medical testing and quarantining of the evacuees. It became apparent within the first 30 minutes of our arrival on Christmas Island that our return flights to Australia which had been pre-booked for us for 6:40 am on 1 February would not be required! We had very quickly turned from the reconnaissance and site-survey team into the advance party.

Our small team of two RAN, two Army and one RAAF personnel very quickly became a highly functional team. We were focused on the mission, communicating regularly and updating Headquarters Joint Operations Command. We quickly formed excellent working relationships with the airport manager, his team and the whole-of-government team led by the Australian Border Force. We were soon also joined by an additional 70 or so ADF personnel.

Together, we received the civilian aircraft carrying Australian expatriates from Wuhan, provided ground transport to a quarantine facility, and then supported those people with accommodation, medical treatment, equipment, rations and communications for approximately three weeks. On arrival at Christmas Island, the majority of the passengers looked incredibly tired and some looked very confused, albeit thankful to have arrived at their (almost) final destination.

Balancing the mission with the desire to provide the Christmas Island locals with enough information to ensure they felt safe was very challenging. We did not understand the complexity of COVID-19 or just how catastrophic it would become, so it was vitally important that we adhered to medical directions. This was very challenging for the medical team as they were operating with limited experience with this virus. Despite these challenges, the support we received was amazing.

My role as the air liaison officer was to manage the baggage crew and provide immediate updates on all flights to the operations cell, including oversight of and assistance with any issues that arose. Prior to and post aircraft tasking, my role included communicating the military aircraft timings and requirements with the airport manager and ground handling manager, managing the air load team, ensuring information exchange and efficiencies were consistent and timely, and providing RAAF operations guidance to the deputy commander, whole-of-government personnel and airport employees.

Without doubt, the highlights of the mission for me were the one-team approach, the regular communication and the desire of every single person to provide support and assistance, no matter how difficult the situation.

Ever since I was a young child, I have heard the media promote the vision of 'the Australian way'. Whenever I play a part in an HADR mission, I am reminded of what that statement means to me: it means getting the job done, no matter the challenges or the difficulties. It means helping your neighbour and working together to achieve a common goal, and it may mean getting yourself dirty or having to face harm. Not all HADR operations may go exactly to plan but, in the end, those people receiving the assistance and relief are typically immensely grateful.[32]

After Operation *COVID-19 Assist* was officially stood up as an ADF operation, the RAAF transported many ADF members as well as civilians to help fight the pandemic in roles including controlling access across state borders and guarding civilians who were in hotel quarantine.

Army personnel boarding a RAAF C-130J Hercules bound for Melbourne prior to serving during Operation *COVID-19 Assist* in 2020 (Defence)

Other personnel

When the immediate disaster is over – when the earthquake aftershocks have stopped, the floodwaters have stopped rising, or the bushfire has been contained – the ADF often transports recovery personnel via air to help with the clean-up effort or to restore critical infrastructure and to rebuild communities. This community service is a Defence tradition which dates back several decades. In just one early mission, after Tropical Cyclone *Brigette* destroyed Port Vila, the capital of New Hebrides (now known as Vanuatu) in 1959, the RAAF transported engineers from the Army via C-130 Hercules to help rebuild the battered city.[33] More than six decades later, recovery and restoration are still core ADF HADR functions. In just a single example from 2016, after Severe Tropical Cyclone *Winston* made landfall in Fiji, the RAN and RAAF transported 1,000 ADF personnel to assist with the rebuilding effort. As part of Operation *Fiji Assist 2016*, these personnel restored electricity to four villages and water facilities to 700 people, and made emergency repairs to nine schools, three medical centres, five community centres and four churches.[34]

Army personnel disembarking a RAAF C-17 at Nausori International Airport in support of Operation *Fiji Assist 2016* (Defence)

Often following a man-made disaster, an investigation will be conducted to try to determine its cause, to put systems in place to prevent similar disasters from occurring in the future. Notable recent examples have followed aviation incidents. When tasked by the Australian Government, the ADF will transport both Australian and foreign personnel to a disaster location to investigate the circumstances that contributed to the disaster. Following the crash of Airlines PNG Flight 4684 in 2009, the ADF transported a victim-identification team and air-accident investigators from the Australian Federal Police to Papua New Guinea. Their task was to identify the 13 passengers and crew who were on board, all of whom had lost their lives, and to investigate the cause of the accident to help prevent future incidents.[35] RAAF officer Wing Commander David Howard noted during Operation *Kokoda Assist*:

> We all understood the urgency and priority of the task at hand. Everyone worked tirelessly to ensure we got the aircraft [transporting the Australian Federal Police team] in the air as soon as possible.[36]

The ADF embarked on a similar mission during Operation *Bring Them Home,* following the crash of Malaysia Airlines Flight 17 in Ukraine in 2014. RAAF Hercules and Globemaster crews flew two missions each day to transport Australian and Dutch police between their operating base in the Netherlands and the crash site in Ukraine, where they investigated the cause of the disaster.[37]

Less commonly, the ADF will transport personnel in support of peacekeeping and political causes, in the hope of preventing future unrest and conflict. This was the case during Operation *Aslan* in 2013 when the RAAF operated eight C-17 and two C-130 flights to transport United Nations personnel to South Sudan during its civil war.[38] Similarly, during Operation *Kimba* in 2022, a RAAF C-17 transported 130 ADF personnel to Papua New Guinea – at the request of its government – to help support its national election through planning, logistics and air transport. As part of this mission, RAAF C-27 Spartan and C-130 Hercules aircraft flew sorties throughout the nation, carrying election material as well as support personnel.[39]

An Army Aviation loadmaster and an Australian Federal Police forensic officer preparing to depart from the Airlines PNG Flight 4684 crash site in Papua New Guinea during Operation *Kokoda Assist* in 2009 (Defence)

The ADF will also occasionally transport politicians and dignitaries to share goodwill and to strengthen ties with nations which have experienced a disaster. During Operation *Pakistan Assist I*, following the Kashmir earthquake in 2005, the Australian Army transported United States politicians and other officials to the affected region via Black Hawk helicopters.[40] Here, they expressed their empathy and willingness to assist Pakistan in its recovery effort. In a similar mission during Operation *Philippines Assist* following Typhoon *Haiyan/Yolanda* in 2013, the RAAF transported almost 200 officials to the disaster area to observe the devastation firsthand and to assure the affected locals of their ongoing assistance.[41]

II. Commercial airlines transporting personnel

Qantas also has a long history of transporting personnel with specific skillsets to the sites of disasters. While the vast majority of these personnel travel via scheduled commercial flights, when the disaster is especially severe or large numbers of personnel are required, the airline will transport them via dedicated relief flights. Following the 2002 Bali bombings, Qantas transported two of its own doctors and three nurses to Indonesia to help treat victims, along with 16 medical specialists from Emergency Management Australia.[42] In a similar mission, after the Boxing Day tsunami in 2004, Qantas transported medical teams to the worst-affected areas via three dedicated relief flights.[43]

Qantas will also transport disaster-mitigation personnel to attempt to minimise the effects of disasters while they are still unfolding. During the devastating 2019–20 Australian bushfire season, Qantas flew thousands of firefighters around the nation to assist with the large-scale firefighting effort. And during the COVID-19 pandemic, Qantas frequently transported medical personnel around Australia, including those from its own medical team, to assist with the treatment of patients.[44]

A member of the Qantas medical team and a doctor from the Australian Medical Assistance Team taking a breather during the COVID-19 pandemic in 2020 (Qantas)

PART III
AUSTRALIAN AIR POWER IN HUMANITARIAN AID AND DISASTER RELIEF INTO THE FUTURE

The future need for humanitarian aid and disaster relief

Despite many advances around the world during the past several decades – improvements in healthcare, food security, standards of living, and more – there will always exist a global need for humanitarian aid and disaster relief (HADR). The key reason for this is simply because disasters and crises will always continue to occur. In 2018, international-development organisation Development Initiatives estimated that more than 206 million people worldwide were in need of HADR at that point in time.[1] In 2021, the Office for the Coordination of Humanitarian Affairs (OCHA) estimated this figure had risen to 235 million people.[2] These statistics continue to trend ever upwards.[3]

Many disasters and crises, such as the disappearance of Malaysia Airlines Flight 370 (MH370) over the Indian Ocean in 2014, were unanticipated and remain unexplained. If it is difficult to prepare for an unexpected event, it is virtually impossible to prepare for an unexplained one. After all, using the case of MH370 as an example, on which aspects should future-risk analysts focus?

- The motivations and psychological health of pilots (if the aircraft crashed due to an act of sabotage by one or both pilots)?
- Security practices at the airport (if the aircraft crashed due to an act of terrorism by a passenger or other party)?
- The provision of oxygen or the presence of contaminants on board (if the aircraft crashed due to the asphyxiation or poisoning of the pilots)?
- The on-board technology (if the aircraft crashed due to malfunctioning equipment)?

This is just the start of a very long list. Even if all of the potential risks could be identified and prioritised, a wide chasm must be bridged to significantly reduce, let alone remove, them. Even expected disasters, such as cyclones which meteorologists have closely tracked from their earliest hours, may have unexpected outcomes for which nations cannot prepare. Immediately after the massive earthquake off the coast of Japan in 2011, by using historical precedents and future forecasting to predict an expected outcome, the Japan Meteorological Agency issued a tsunami warning. But the meltdown of the Fukushima Daiichi Nuclear Power Plant was unexpected. This may be an extreme example, but there are dozens of others. A cyclone can trigger a flood which can kill crops and livestock which can create a famine. A famine can cause civil unrest which can lead to military intervention which can trigger terrorism. But to avoid being overwhelmed by endless theoretical and low-chance possibilities, it is wisest for nations that engage in HADR, such as Australia, to prepare for the *most likely* of these disasters and crises, while remaining adaptable and rapidly responsive to any unexpected outcomes. In other words, to prepare for the cyclone but also have a plan for the famine; and to prepare for the famine but also have a plan for the terrorism.

Australia's role in humanitarian aid and disaster relief into the future

To best plan its future HADR efforts, it is both valuable and wise for Australia to examine statistical data. The following trends provide an overview. The Asia–Pacific region experiences more disasters than any other region in the world.[4] These disasters may be attributed to the region's varying topography (which may be susceptible to earthquakes, tsunamis and so on), its climates (which may regularly cause cyclones, floods and other weather-based disasters), its dense population (which may contribute to food shortages, epidemics and more), and its many religions and systems of government (which may lead to civil unrest, terrorism and other violence) – along with the complex interplay of all of these. Further, the world's nine largest megacities are located in Asia, and more than 30% of the world's urban population live in slums in the Asia–Pacific region.[5] In 2017, the United Nations reported that a person who lives in the Asia–Pacific region is five times more likely to be affected by a natural disaster than a person who lives outside of that region.[6] Consequently, nations in the Asia–Pacific region frequently and consistently have the greatest need, out of all of the regions in the world, for HADR.[7] This means Australia – in line with its long-standing tradition of helping others, as well as to promote regional stability and prosperity – will almost certainly continue to engage in HADR into the future.[8] The Australian Council for International Development states:

> Australia has a proud history of providing lifesaving assistance to people affected by humanitarian crises, playing a pivotal role in advancing the rules-based international order and advocating for conflict prevention, conflict resolution and peace building at the international level.[9]

Recognising the value of air power in HADR missions, the Australian Government will likely continue to task the Australian Defence Force (ADF), along with commercial airlines, to conduct HADR throughout the Asia–Pacific region and beyond. The Royal Australian Navy (RAN), Australian Army and Royal Australian Air Force (RAAF) will continue to use their aircraft and unique professional and operational capabilities to engage in HADR. They will continue to deliver and airdrop relief supplies, conduct evacuation and aeromedical-evacuation flights, engage in aerial search-and-rescue and aerial damage-assessment missions, repatriate the bodies of Australians, and transport personnel to provide HADR.

Yet with the rise of new and enhanced aviation technologies, the ADF will expand its intelligence, surveillance and reconnaissance capabilities. The MQ-4C Triton Unmanned Aircraft System, for example, will support Australia's future search-and-rescue and damage-assessment capabilities. This and other new and developing technologies will have particular value within the complex socio-political theatre of the disaster-prone Asia–Pacific region. They will be able to equip Australia with the necessary intelligence to attempt to prevent looming crises such as political revolutions and wars, track natural events such as cyclones in their earliest stages, and minimise, through aerial search and rescue and aerial damage assessment, the impact of disasters after they have occurred. For the ADF, intelligence will inform its future strategy, and its future strategy will inform its future HADR efforts.

Commercial airlines will continue to contribute to HADR efforts alongside, and even at times instead of, the ADF. They will most likely continue to deliver relief supplies, conduct evacuations, transport personnel to disaster sites and even, in unique circumstances, repatriate the bodies of Australians.

In these ways, the air power of both the ADF and commercial airlines will continue to be a key enabler of Australia's HADR efforts into the future.

Australia as a good international citizen

As Part I of this book explored, in addition to helping others and promoting national interests, one of the reasons why contemporary democratic nations such as Australia often choose to engage in HADR is to promote good international relations. This will likely continue into the future. When Australian men and women – whether military personnel, public officials or civilians – engage in HADR in the future, the international community will continue to regard them as being ambassadors for Australia. The uniforms and aircraft livery used by the RAN, Army, RAAF and commercial airlines – especially the distinctive kangaroo logos used by Qantas and all three ADF services – will continue to announce to the world that, in times of need, Australia comes to help.

The historical record is full of examples of individuals and nations who have identified Australia as a source of help during a time of need. In fact, those at the highest levels of a nation's political and military systems have acknowledged Australia's assistance in the past. During Operation *Philippines Assist* in 2013, when Australia established a field hospital to treat those who were injured by Typhoon *Haiyan/Yolanda*, former General Roy Deveraturda from the Armed Forces of the Philippines stated: 'We will never forget the assistance from Australia.'[10] More frequently, the feedback is less formal and more spontaneous. As RAAF pilot Flight Lieutenant Luke Ridgway observed when he was delivering relief supplies to South Sudan during Operation *Aslan* in 2013: 'The response on the ground has been amazing. Big smiles when they see it's an Australian plane.'[11]

In the future, despite the challenges and often confronting circumstances inherent in almost all HADR missions, the men and women who provide aid on behalf of Australia will likely continue to regard their involvement as a privilege far beyond any call of duty. When the RAAF evacuated hospital patients from harm's way during Operation *Yasi Assist* in 2011, Group Captain Don Sutherland noted: 'We never have any problems in motivating the crews to do these sort of things.'[12] Similarly, the officer in charge of the HADR mission in Western Australia following Severe Tropical Cyclone *Seroja* in 2021, Flight Lieutenant Kyle Hornberg, stated: 'Our squadron is often at its best when it's supporting humanitarian aid and disaster relief operations.'[13]

The Australian spirit of mateship is truly apparent when men and women, both military personnel and civilians, engage in HADR despite a genuine risk to their lives. The crew on the Qantas flight to evacuate Australian nationals from Wuhan in China in the early days of the COVID-19 pandemic had all volunteered to take part, despite the risks to their health and lives if they should contract the virus.[14] The former chief executive officer of Qantas, Alan Joyce, reflected: 'They are inspirational because they have done this to help Australians in need.'[15]

CONCLUSION

This book has made a contribution to the growing appreciation of Australia's use of airborne humanitarian aid and disaster relief (HADR), both historically and today. It has explored the role of Australian air power in HADR since the Second World War: how Australia has used both military and commercial aircraft to provide assistance to those in need, both overseas and within its own borders.

Part I showed that, historically, nations and empires engaged in HADR for political, philosophical/religious and – since relatively recently – altruistic reasons. It demonstrated that today, while many nations engage in HADR for altruistic reasons, they also do so in an attempt to safeguard or to promote their national and political interests. Part I further explored the role of the military in HADR both throughout history and today and demonstrated that the default response for many governments who engage in HADR, including Australia, is to task their militaries to provide this activity.

Part II explored the different air-power tactics the Australian Defence Force (ADF) and Australian commercial airlines have used to provide HADR since the Second World War, right up to the present day. It demonstrated that all three ADF services – the Royal Australian Navy, the Australian Army and the Royal Australian Air Force (RAAF) – can and do provide Australia's military aviation HADR capability, while Australia's flagship airline, Qantas, has historically been the predominant HADR provider among Australia's commercial airlines. Especially memorable in this section were the first-hand accounts by ADF members of their personal involvement in HADR missions. Their stories acknowledge their privilege of having been involved in lifesaving and life-honouring humanitarian work. Part II firstly explored how both the ADF and Qantas deliver relief supplies throughout the Asia–Pacific region and the world, ever since Qantas's delivery of food parcels to Great Britain during its inaugural Sydney-to-London flight in 1947. It then explored the ADF's capability to airdrop supplies, using the example of Operation *Okra* in 2014 when the RAAF airdropped relief supplies from a C-130J Hercules to Yazidi refugees on Mount Sinjar in Iraq. It then showed how both the ADF and Qantas evacuate at-risk and injured people from the sites of conflict and natural disasters, including when Qantas broke the world record for carrying the largest number of people (674 passengers plus 23 crewmembers) on a Boeing 747, after Cyclone *Tracy* hit Darwin in 1974. This section next explored how the ADF uses its air power to search disaster zones for survivors, including when it searched for missing airliner MH370 in 2014 during the joint search-and-rescue mission Operation *Southern Indian Ocean*. After touching on aerial damage-assessment missions, this section explored how both the ADF and Qantas may be tasked to repatriate the bodies of Australians who have lost their lives in disasters overseas, such as the 88 Australians who were killed during the 2002 Bali bombings. The final section explored how both the ADF and Qantas may transport personnel with specific professional skillsets to provide HADR. It showed that sometimes these are not only *person*nel: during Operation *Pacific Assist 2011*, following the Tōhoku earthquake, tsunami and Fukushima Daiichi Nuclear Power Plant meltdown in 2011, the RAAF transported search-and-rescue dogs who became 'the most famous dogs in Japan'.

Lastly, Part III of this book explored why Australia is likely to continue to engage in HADR in the future. It explained that the Asia–Pacific region experiences more disasters than any other region in the world, and that air power will almost certainly play a central role in Australia's future HADR efforts. It touched on new and emerging aviation technologies which the ADF may use in its future HADR missions, including advanced intelligence, surveillance and reconnaissance capabilities. Finally, this section concluded by predicting that the Australian men and women who engage in HADR in the future will continue to be regarded by the international community as ambassadors for Australia.

If it is possible to distil the significance of the role of Australian air power in HADR missions into just a few words, Vanuatu citizen Sulia Manaroto may well have succeeded during Operation *Pacific Assist 2015*, following Severe Tropical Cyclone *Pam*: 'Australia was the first to arrive in Vanuatu to provide help. It shows the Australians have big hearts.'[1]

ACKNOWLEDGEMENTS

My warmest thanks and heartfelt gratitude to everyone who assisted me in writing this book. Most of all:

Thank you to Professor Sanu Kainikara and the team at the RAAF's Air and Space Power Centre, who first started me on this journey.

Thank you to Air Vice-Marshal (retd) Tracy Smart who wrote the wonderful foreword and who every day inspires other Australian women to aim high.

Thank you to the men and women of the ADF who so generously shared their personal HADR experiences with me. Your accounts have truly brought to life all of the challenges and highlights, the tragedies and triumphs, inherent in HADR missions.

From the Royal Australian Navy:

- Captain Jace Hutchison
- Petty Officer Scott Broughton

From the Australian Army:

- Colonel Phil Baldoni

From the Royal Australian Air Force:

- Air Commodore Craig Heap
- Air Commodore Tony McCormack
- Group Captain Roger McCutcheon
- Wing Commander Stuart Wheal
- Squadron Leader Kevin Auld
- Squadron Leader Cameron Brockel
- Squadron Leader David Weekley
- Flight Lieutenant Cale Barnes
- Flying Officer Jorge Elosegui Guerra
- Warrant Officer Shaunn Segon
- Sergeant Jacquelyn Nelson
- Corporal Deniele Oehm
- Leading Aircraftman Sam Schmidt

From the list above, I must single out Air Commodore Tony McCormack who generously provided two wonderful first-hand accounts and then also worked with me to dramatise one of them as the prologue. Sir, your memory of events after 25 years is truly enviable.

Thank you to the team at History and Heritage – Air Force, who helped to transform my manuscript into the finished book you now hold. Most of all, thank you to Group Captain Lewis Frederickson for your literary mentorship, Rosalind Turner for your eagle-eyed fact checking and Corporal Steven Hobbs for creating the maps.

And, finally, thank you to my loved ones, who shared the ups and downs of writing this book – as well as a bottle or two of champagne.

Karyn Markwell
December 2024

Appendix A
MILITARY OPERATIONS INCLUDED IN THIS BOOK

Berlin Airlift
Berlin Blockade, Germany, 1948–49

Operation *Ashika Assist*
Princess Ashika sinking, Tonga, 2009

Operation *Aslan*
South Sudanese Civil War, South Sudan, 2013

Operation *Babylift*
Vietnam War, Vietnam, 1975

Operation *Bad Water*
Malaysia flood, Malaysia, 1967

Operation *Bali Assist*
2002 Bali bombings, Indonesia

Operation *Bring Them Home*
Crash of Malaysia Airlines Flight 17, Ukraine, 2014

Operation *Bushfire Assist*
Australian bushfires, Australia, 2019–20

Operation *Bushranger*
Kashmir earthquake, Pakistan, 2006

Operation *Carnelian*
Civil unrest, Sudan, 2023

Operation *Christchurch Assist*
2011 Christchurch earthquake, New Zealand

Operation *COVID-19 Assist*
COVID-19 pandemic, worldwide, 2020–22

Operation *Fiji Assist 2016*
Severe Tropical Cyclone *Winston*, Fiji, 2016

Operation *Fiji Assist 2020*
Cyclone *Yasa*, Fiji

Operation *Flood Assist*
Nationwide flooding, Australia, 2022–23

Operation *Kimba*
National election, Papua New Guinea, 2022

Operation *Kokoda Assist*
Crash of Airlines PNG Flight 4684, Papua New Guinea, 2009

Operation *Lilia*
Civil unrest, Solomon Islands, 2021–22

Operation *Longreach*
Kashmir earthquake, Pakistan, 2006

Operation *Navy Help Darwin*
Cyclone *Tracy*, Australia, 1974

Operation *Nepal Assist*
Gorkha earthquake, Nepal, 2015

Operation *Okra*
Genocide of Yazidis, Iraq, 2014

Operation *Pacific Assist 2011*
Tōhoku earthquake, tsunami and Fukushima Daiichi Nuclear Power Plant meltdown, Japan

Operation *Pakistan Assist I*
Kashmir earthquake, Pakistan, 2005–06

Operation *Philippines Assist*
Typhoon *Haiyan/Yolanda*, The Philippines, 2013

Operation *Queensland Flood Assist*
Queensland floods, Australia, 2010–13

Operation *Ramp*
Lebanon War, Lebanon, 2006

Operation *Southern Indian Ocean*
Disappearance of Malaysia Airlines Flight 370, Indian Ocean, 2014

Operation *Spitfire*
East Timorese fight for independence, East Timor, 1999

Operation *Sumatra Assist I*
Boxing Day tsunami, Southeast Asia, 2004–05

Operation *Sumatra Assist II*
2005 Nias–Simeulue earthquake, Indonesia

Operation *Tonga Assist 2022*
Eruption of Hunga Tonga–Hunga Ha'apai volcano, Tonga

Operation *Vanuatu Assist 2023*
Tropical Cyclones *Judy* and *Kevin*, Vanuatu

Operation *Vista*
Cambodian coup, Cambodia, 1997

Operation *Yasi Assist*
Severe Tropical Cyclone *Yasi*, Australia, 2011

Appendix B

MILITARY AIRCRAFT INCLUDED IN THIS BOOK

Airbus KC-30A Multi-Role Tanker Transport
RAAF: No 33 Squadron
Dates in service: 2013–present
Total number of aircraft: 7

Lockheed AP-3C Orion
RAAF: No 10 Squadron, No 11 Squadron
Dates in service: 2002–23
Total number of aircraft: 18

Vertol/Boeing CH-47C/D/F Chinook
Army: 5th Aviation Regiment
RAAF: No 12 Squadron
Dates in service (Army): 1995–present
Dates in service (RAAF): 1974–89
Total number of aircraft: 34

Boeing C-17A Globemaster III
RAAF: No 36 Squadron
Dates in service: 2006–present
Total number of aircraft: 8

Alenia C-27J Spartan
RAAF: No 35 Squadron
Dates in service: 2015–present
Total number of aircraft: 10

Lockheed C-130A Hercules
RAAF: No 36 Squadron
Dates in service: 1959–78
Total number of aircraft: 12

Lockheed C-130E Hercules
RAAF: No 37 Squadron
Dates in service: 1966–99
Total number of aircraft: 12

Lockheed C-130H Hercules
RAAF: No 36 Squadron, No 37 Squadron
Dates in service: 1978–2012
Total number of aircraft: 12

Lockheed Martin C-130J Hercules
RAAF: No 37 Squadron
Dates in service: 1999–present
Total number of aircraft: 12; 20 on order

de Havilland DH.98 Mosquito
RAAF: several units and squadrons, including No 1 Photographic Reconnaissance Unit
Dates in service: 1944–55
Total number of aircraft: 209

Douglas C-47 Dakota
RAAF: No 10 Squadron, No 36 Squadron, No 38 Squadron
Dates in service: 1943–73
Total number of aircraft: 124

Boeing E-7A Wedgetail
RAAF: No 2 Squadron
Dates in service: 2009–present
Total number of aircraft: 6

Hawker Siddeley HS748
RAN: 851 Squadron, 723 Squadron
Dates in service: 1973–2000
Total number of aircraft: 2

NHI Industries MRH-90 Taipan
Army: 5th Aviation Regiment, 6th Aviation Regiment
RAN: 808 Squadron
Dates in service: 2005–24
Total number of aircraft: 46

Sikorsky MH-60R Seahawk
RAN: 816 Squadron, 725 Squadron
Dates in service: 2013–present
Total number of aircraft: 24; 12 on order

Sikorsky S-70B Seahawk
RAN: 816 Squadron
Dates in service: 1989–2017
Total number of aircraft: 16

Lockheed P-3C Orion
RAAF: No 10 Squadron
Dates in service: 1978–2005
Total number of aircraft: 1

Boeing P-8A Poseidon
RAAF: No 11 Squadron
Dates in service: 2016–present
Total number of aircraft: 12; 2 on order

Sikorsky S-70A Black Hawk
Army: 5th Aviation Regiment
Dates in service: 1989–2021
Total number of aircraft: 39

Westland Sea King Mk.50/50A
RAN: 817 Squadron
Dates in service: 1974–2011
Total number of aircraft: 12

Westland Wessex 31B
RAN: 725 Squadron, 817 Squadron
Dates in service: 1968–89
Total number of aircraft: 23

BIBLIOGRAPHY

Published works

Bullard, Steven, *In Their Time of Need: Australia's overseas emergency relief operations, 1918–2006*, Cambridge University Press, Cambridge, 2017.

Commonwealth of Australia, *ADF Air Power*, Air and Space Power Centre, Canberra, 2023.

——, *Australian Air Publication 1000–D—The Air Power Manual*, 6th edn, Air Power Development Centre, Canberra, 2013.

——, *Australian Maritime Doctrine: RAN Doctrine 1*, Sea Power Centre – Australia, Canberra, 2010.

——, *Campaigns and Operations*, 3rd edn, Doctrine Directorate, Canberra, 2023.

——, *Stabilisation and Humanitarian Operations*, Doctrine Directorate, Canberra, 2023.

Joint Chiefs of Staff, *Joint Publication 3-29—Foreign Humanitarian Assistance*, Joint Force Development, Washington, 2019.

Lax, Mark, *Taking the Lead: The Royal Australian Air Force 1972–1996*, Simon and Schuster, Cammeray, 2020.

Ministry of Defence, *Joint Doctrine Publication 3-52—Disaster Relief Operations Overseas: the Military Contribution*, 3rd edn, Development, Concepts and Doctrine Centre, Swindon, 2016.

North Atlantic Treaty Organization, *Allied Joint Doctrine for the Military Contribution to Humanitarian Assistance*, NATO Standardization Office, Brussels, 2015.

O'Brien, Graham, *Always There: A History of Air Force Combat Support*, Air Power Development Centre, Canberra, 2009.

Reports

Parliament of the Commonwealth of Australia, *Review of the Defence Annual Report 2003–04*, Joint Standing Committee on Defence, Foreign Affairs and Trade, Canberra, 2005.

Qantas Airways Limited, *2003 Qantas Annual Report*, Qantas Airways Limited, Mascot, 2003.

——, *Qantas Annual Report 2005*, Qantas Airways Limited, Mascot, 2005.

Reghenzani, Christine, *Women in the ADF: six decades of policy change (1950 to 2011)*, Department of Parliamentary Services, 2015.

Journal articles

Bastian, Nathaniel D, et al, 'Multi-criteria logistics modeling for military humanitarian assistance and disaster relief aerial delivery operations', *Springer*, 2014, 10(921–53)

Canyon, Deon V, Benjamin J Ryan, and Frederick M Burkle, 'Military Provision of Humanitarian Assistance and Disaster Relief in Non-Conflict Crises', *Journal of Homeland Security and Emergency Management*, November 2017, (1–5).

Cretu, Doina Anca, 'Nationalizing international relief: Romanian responses to American aid for children in the Great War era', *European Review of History: Revue europeenne d'histoire*, 2020, 27:1–2(1–21).

Fuller, Pierre, 'Decentring international and institutional famine relief in late nineteenth-century China: in search of the local', *European Review of History: Revue europeenne d'histoire*, 2015, 22:6(873–89).

Geiselman, Eric E, et al., 'Airdrop guidance display format for precision airdrop application on an auxiliary display equipped aircraft', *The International Journal of Aviation Psychology*, 2015, 25:3–4(141–56).

Kind-Kovács, Friederike, 'The Great War, the child's body and the American Red Cross', *European Review of History: Revue européenne d'histoire*, 2016, 23:1–2(33–62).

Merziger, Patrick, 'The "radical humanism" of "Cap Anamur"/"German Emergency Doctors" in the 1980s: a turning point for the idea, practice and policy of humanitarian aid', *European Review of History: Revue européenne d'histoire*, 2016, 23:1–2(171–92).

Newby, Vanessa, 'ANZUS cooperation in humanitarian assistance and disaster response in the Asia-Pacific: ships in the night?', *Australian Journal of International Affairs*, 2020, 74:1(72–88).

O'Hagan, Jacinta, 'Australia and the promise and the perils of humanitarian diplomacy', *Australian Journal of International Affairs*, 2016, 70:6(657–69).

Roquen, Jeff, 'International law and "humanity" in the making and unmaking of European solidarity, 1830–1915', *European Review of History: Revue europeenne d'histoire*, 2017, 24:6(889–904).

Salvatici, Silvia, '"Fighters without guns": humanitarianism and military action in the aftermath of the Second World War', *European Review of History: Revue europeenne d'histoire*, 2018, 25:6(957–76).

Sasson, Tehila, and James Vernon, 'Practising the British way of famine: technologies of relief, 1770–1985', *European Review of History: Revue europeenne d'histoire* , 2015, 22:6(860–72).

Newspapers and periodicals

ABS Magazine

Air Force News

Army News

Australian Aviation

Weekend Australian

Speeches

McCormack, Tony, 'Air Power in Disaster Relief: The Role of the Royal Australian Air Force in Australia's Response to the 2011 Japanese Earthquake and Tsunami', Canberra, 31 July 2014.

Spender, Percy, 'International affairs', Parliament of Australia, Canberra, 9 March 1950.

Correspondence

Auld, Kevin, email to author, 14 September 2023.

Baldoni, Phil, email to author, 23 May 2023.

Barnes, Cale, email to author, 20 June 2023.

Brockel, Cameron, email to author, 22 May 2023.

Broughton, Scott, email to author, 24 July 2023.

Guerra, Elosegui, email to author, 18 May 2023.

Heap, Craig, email to author, 30 June 2023.

Hutchison, Jace, email to author, 25 June 2023.

McCormack, Tony, emails to author, 22 May 2023, 21 June 2023 and 26 April 2024.

McCutcheon, Roger, email to author, 15 June 2023.

Nelson, Jacquelyn, email to author, 3 July 2023.

Oehm, Deniele, email to author, 1 June 2023.

Segon, Shaunn, email to author, 8 June 2023.

Schmidt, Sam, email to author, 16 June 2023.

Weekley, David, email to author, 23 May 2023.

Wheal, Stuart, email to author, 20 May 2023.

Internet resources

'2006: Lebanon war', *BBC News*, updated 6 May 2008, at http://news.bbc.co.uk/2/hi/middle_east/7381389.stm.

'2019–2020 Australian Bushfires', *Center for Disaster Philanthropy*, updated 17 February 2020, at https://disasterphilanthropy.org/disasters/2019-australian-wildfires/#:~:text=Donations%20to%20the%20CDP%20Global,three%2Dyear%20bushfire%20recovery%20program.

'4 years ago: the genocide against the Yazidis in northern Iraq (August 3, 2014)', *Gesellschaft für bedrohte Völker*, updated 8 February 2018, at https://www.gfbv.de/en/news/4-years-ago-the-genocide-against-the-yazidis-in-northern-iraq-august-3-2014-9323/.

'817 Squadron History', *Royal Australian Navy*, n. d., at https://www.navy.gov.au/history/squadron-histories/817-squadron-history.

'ADF moves to support fire crews', *Australian Defence Magazine*, updated 12 November 2019, at https://www.australiandefence.com.au/news/adf-moves-to-support-fire-crews.

'ADF: past operations in Timor-Leste (East Timor)', *Nautilus Institute*, n. d., at https://nautilus.org/publications/books/australian-forces-abroad/east-timor/adf-past-operations-in-timor-leste-east-timor/.

'Air Mobility Group', *Royal Australian Air Force*, n. d., at https://www.airforce.gov.au/about-us/hq-air-command/air-mobility-group.

'AirAsia QZ8501: Search resumes for missing flight after anxious relatives spend night in crisis centre', *ABC News*, updated 29 December 2014, at https://www.abc.net.au/news/2014-12-29/airasia-flight-qz8501-search-to-resume/5990800.

Aljibe, Ted, 'Philippines: five years after Typhoon Haiyan', *The Guardian*, updated 6 November 2018, at https://www.theguardian.com/artanddesign/2018/nov/06/philippines-five-years-after-typhoon-haiyan.

'Australia doubles NZ quake help', *ABC News*, updated 22 February 2011, at https://www.abc.net.au/news/2011-02-22/australia-doubles-nz-quake-help/1953726.

'Australia's response to the Indian Ocean Tsunami: Report for the Period Ending 30 June 2005', *Parliament of Australia*, n. d., at https://www.dfat.gov.au/about-us/publications/Pages/australia-s-response-to-the-indian-ocean-tsunami-report-for-the-period-ending-30-june-2005.

'Australia's Response to Typhoon Yolanda', *Australian Embassy The Philippines*, n. d., at https://philippines.embassy.gov.au/mnla/TyphoonYolandaTyphoonYolanda.html#:~:text=Australia%27s%20Foreign%20Minister%20Julie%20Bishop,contribution%20to%20A%2430%20million.

'Bali bombings', *National Museum Australia*, n. d., at https://www.nma.gov.au/defining-moments/resources/bali-bombings.

Barkham, Patrick, and Adam Gabbatt, 'Cyclone Yasi strikes North Queensland', *The Guardian*, updated 3 February 2011, at https://www.theguardian.com/world/2011/feb/02/cyclone-yasi-north-queensland.

Bell, Frances, and Evelyn Manfield, 'Passengers on coronavirus evacuation flight from Wuhan land on Christmas Island', *ABC News*, updated 4 February 2020, at https://www.abc.net.au/news/2020-02-03/coronavirus-wuhan-evacuation-flight-reaches-wa-christmas-island/11923324.

'Canberra's airport has reopened after bushfire downgrade', *9News*, updated 23 January 2020, at https://www.9news.com.au/national/canberra-flights-cancelled-delays-bushfire-act-australian-news/a6140738-9be0-41f3-b863-ea8d3da7cb17#:~:text=Canberra%27s%20airport%20has%20reopened%20with,the%20fire%20into%20the%20evening.

Cetorelli, Valeria, et al., 'ISIS' Yazidi Genocide: Demographic Evidence of the Killings and Kidnappings', *Foreign Affairs*, updated 8 June 2017, at https://www.foreignaffairs.com/articles/syria/2017-06-08/isis-yazidi-genocide.

'Coronavirus rescue flights secured for Australians stranded in Peru, Argentina and South Africa', *SBS News*, updated 10 April 2020, at https://www.sbs.com.au/news/article/coronavirus-rescue-flights-secured-for-australians-stranded-in-peru-argentina-and-south-africa/sfd3fsi61.

'Country profile – Vietnam', *Department of Home Affairs*, updated 22 July 2020, at https://www.homeaffairs.gov.au/research-and-statistics/statistics/country-profiles/profiles/vietnam.

Cuny, Frederick C, 'Use of the Military in Humanitarian relief', *Frontline*, updated November 1989, at https://www.pbs.org/wgbh/pages/frontline/shows/cuny/laptop/humanrelief.html#:~:text=To%20date%2C%20the%20most%20common,of%20the%20Red%20Cross%20(ICRC).

'Cyclone Tracy, 1974', *Knowledge Hub*, n. d., at https://knowledge.aidr.org.au/resources/cyclone-cyclone-tracy-darwin-1974/.

'Cyclone Tracy', *Library & Archives NT*, n. d., at https://lant.nt.gov.au/explore-nt-history/cyclone-tracy.

'Devastated survivor describes Tongan ferry tragedy', *The Sydney Morning Herald*, updated 8 August 2009, at https://www.smh.com.au/world/devastated-survivor-describes-tongan-ferry-tragedy-20090808-edeo.html.

di Stefano, Mark, and Stephen McDonell, 'Typhoon Haiyan: Australian emergency medical team heads for Philippines', *ABC News*, updated 13 November 2013, at https://www.abc.net.au/news/2013-11-13/raaf-aircraft-prepare-to-fly-to-philippines-medical-team-typhoo/5088470.

'Berlin Airlift', *Digger History*, n. d., at http://www.diggerhistory.info/pages-battles/berlin-airlift.htm.

'Disaster relief - Cyclone Tracy and Tasman Bridge', *Sea Power Centre Australia*, updated December 2004, at https://www.navy.gov.au/history/feature-histories/disaster-relief-cyclone-tracy-and-tasman-bridge#:~:text=Between%201%20and%2030%20January,commercial%20buildings%20and%20recreational%20facilities.

Doran, Matthew, 'RAAF rescue mission evacuates 36 Australians and their family members from Sudan', *ABC News*, updated 3 May 2023, at https://www.abc.net.au/news/2023-05-03/australian-rescue-mission-flight-out-of-sudan/102295460.

Dougherty, Robert, 'Fire and Rescue NSW firefighters are being transported by Royal Australian Air Force planes to help battle the South Coast fires', *Port News*, updated 6 January 2020, at https://www.portnews.com.au/story/6567808/mid-north-coast-firefighters-deployed-to-nations-southern-frontline/.

Dziedzic, Stephen, 'About 900 Australians stuck in COVID-hit India and wanting to return now listed as "vulnerable", High Commissioner says', *ABC News*, updated 6 May 2021, at https://www.abc.net.au/news/2021-05-05/australians-health-high-commission-india-supplies-covid-19/100117620.

'Egypt Uprising of 2011', *Encyclopaedia Britannica*, n. d., at https://www.britannica.com/event/Egypt-Uprising-of-2011.

'Fit for the future: Priorities for Australia's humanitarian action', *Australian Council for International Development*, updated 17 February 2020, at https://acfid.asn.au/acfid-releases-guidance-for-the-development-of-a-disability-inclusion-policy-3-15/.

Greene, Andrew, 'Nepal earthquake: Aid, RAAF medical evacuation teams on way to Nepal but ADF aircraft still unable to land', *ABC News*, updated 29 April 2015, at https://www.abc.net.au/news/2015-04-29/australian-defence-aircraft-still-unable-to-land-in-nepal/6430802.

Heanue, Siobhan, 'Nepal earthquake: First Australians evacuated from Kathmandu on board RAAF transport planes', *ABC News*, updated 1 May 2015, at https://www.abc.net.au/news/2015-05-01/nepal-aid-reaches-earthquake-zone-australians-evacuated/6436476.

'Humanitarian preparedness and response', *Department of Foreign Affairs and Trade*, n. d., at https://www.dfat.gov.au/development/topics/development-issues/building-resilience/humanitarian-preparedness-and-response.

'Humanitarian Principles', United Nations Office for the Coordination of Humanitarian Affairs, New York, 2022, at https://www.unocha.org/publications/report/world/ocha-message-humanitarian-principles-enar.

'Humanitarian support', *Royal Australian Air Force*, n. d., at https://www.airforce.gov.au/our-work/humanitarian-support.

'Indian Ocean tsunami', *Department of Foreign Affairs and Trade*, updated 19 December 2014, at https://www.dfat.gov.au/news/news/Pages/indian-ocean-tsunami.

'Infographic: Nepal earthquake – Australian Government humanitarian response', *Department of Foreign Affairs and Trade*, updated 19 December 2019, at https://www.dfat.gov.au/news/news/Pages/nepal-earthquake-australian-government-humanitarian-response#:~:text=Infographic%3A%20Nepal%20earthquake%20%2D%20Australian%20Government%20humanitarian%20response,-19%20December%202019&text=The%20Australian%20Government%20has%20provided,million%20in%20lifesaving%20humanitarian%20support.

'Iraq crisis: Australian plane drops humanitarian aid into Amerli residents under siege by Islamic State militants', *ABC News*, updated 31 August 2014, at https://www.abc.net.au/news/2014-08-31/australian-planes-drop-humanitarian-aid-into-iraq/5708636.

Marks, Kathy, 'Qantas celebrates 60 years of the "Kangaroo Route"', *The Independent*, updated 30 November 2007, at https://www.independent.co.uk/news/world/australasia/qantas-celebrates-60-years-of-the-kangaroo-route-761078.html.

McLaughlin, Andrew, 'Operation Bushfire Assist: The Australian Defence Force Responds', *SLDinfo.com*, updated 13 January 2020, at https://sldinfo.com/2020/01/operation-bushfire-assist-the-australian-defence-force-responds/.

'MH17 airbridge to Ukraine "smashing it"', *SBS News*, updated 31 July 2014, at https://www.sbs.com.au/news/article/mh17-airbridge-to-ukraine-smashing-it/l89pd9u1q.

'MH17 Ukraine plane crash: What we know', *BBC News*, updated 26 February 2020, at https://www.bbc.com/news/world-europe-28357880.

Millar, Paul, 'Kokoda crash victims arrive home', *Sydney Morning Herald*, updated 26 August 2009, at https://www.smh.com.au/national/kokoda-crash-victims-arrive-home-20090826-eyyc.html.

'Minister for Defence – Operation Pacific Assist Update', *The Hon Kevin Andrews MP*, updated 20 March 2015, at https://www.minister.defence.gov.au/media-releases/2015-03-17/minister-defence-operation-pacific-assist-update.

Nachemson, Andrew, 'Was Cambodia Ever Really a Democracy?', *The Diplomat*, updated 4 July 2019, at https://thediplomat.com/2019/07/was-cambodia-ever-really-a-democracy/.

Newborn, Jaime, 'Aircraft heading to cyclone zone', *The Courier Mail*, updated 4 February 2011, at https://www.couriermail.com.au/news/queensland/mackay/aircraft-heading-to-cyclone-zone/news-story/99a7724772f5cbf7dacae1bbb306f76f.

'Operation Babylift', *Anzac Portal*, n. d., at https://anzacportal.dva.gov.au/wars-and-missions/vietnam-war-1962-1975/royal-australian-air-force/raaf-1975#1.

'Operation Fiji Assist widens - LHD deployed,' *Australian Defence Magazine*, updated 24 February 2016, at https://www.australiandefence.com.au/news/operation-fiji-assist-widens-lhd-deployed.

'Operation Nepal Assist 2015', *Department of Defence*, n. d., at https://www.airforce.gov.au/about-us/history/our-journey/operation-nepal-assist#:~:text=Following%20a%20devastating%20earthquake%20on,other%20foreign%20nationals%20to%20Thailand.

'Operation Ramp', *Australian War Memorial*, n. d., at https://www.awm.gov.au/collection/LIB100011631.

'Operation Ramp', *Migrants in Countries in Crisis*, n. d., at https://micicinitiative.iom.int/operation-ramp-0.

O'Sullivan, Matt, 'Virgin in bid to unseat Qantas as Australia's chief airline for "rescue" flights', *The Sydney Morning Herald*, updated 13 December 2013, at https://www.smh.com.au/business/virgin-in-bid-to-unseat-qantas-as-australias-chief-airline-for-rescue-flights-20131212-2za5c.html.

'Our community', *Qantas*, n. d., at https://www.qantas.com/au/en/qantas-group/acting-responsibly/our-community.html.

'Our history', *Qantas*, n. d., at https://www.qantas.com/au/en/about-us/our-company/our-history.html.

Penberthy, Natsumi, 'On this day in history: 2004 Boxing Day tsunami', *Australian Geographic*, updated 18 December 2014, at https://www.australiangeographic.com.au/blogs/on-this-day/2014/12/on-this-day-in-history-boxing-day-tsunami/.

'Qantas Milestones and Transactions', *Qantas*, updated November 2015, at https://investor.qantas.com/home/?page=milestones-and-transactions.

'Qantas offers free flights for Aussies in Egypt', *ABC News*, updated 2 February 2011, at https://www.abc.net.au/news/2011-02-02/qantas-offers-free-flights-for-aussies-in-egypt/1927462.

'RAAF advances airdrop capability', *Australian Defence Magazine*, updated 26 August 2015, at https://www.australiandefence.com.au/news/raaf-advances-airdrop-capability#:~:text=The%20RAAF%20has%20advanced%20its,zone%20by%20using%20steerable%20parachutes.

Reid, Kathryn, '2011 Japan earthquake and tsunami: Facts, FAQs, and how to help', *World Vision*, updated 7 May 2019, at https://www.worldvision.org/disaster-relief-news-stories/2011-japan-earthquake-and-tsunami-facts#:~:text=Fast%20facts%3A%202011%20Japan%20earthquake%20and%20tsunami,-The%20T%C5%8Dhoku%20earthquake&text=At%20%24360%20billion%2C%20the%20earthquake,from%20drowning%20during%20the%20tsunami.

Reid, Kathryn, '2015 Cyclone Pam: Facts, FAQs, and how to help', *World Vision*, updated 3 July 2018, at https://www.worldvision.org/disaster-relief-news-stories/2015-vanuatu-cyclone-pam-facts#:~:text=Cyclone%20Pam%20struck%20Vanuatu%20as,affected%20areas%20were%20wiped%20out.

'Rescue flight brings Vietnamese orphans out of Saigon', *Anzac Portal*, updated 16 November 2022, at https://anzacportal.dva.gov.au/stories/australians-wartime/rescue-flight-brings-vietnamese-orphans-out-saigon.

Scott, Irene, 'South Sudan crisis: Former ABC journalist Irene Scott travels with RAAF crew on relief mission', *ABC News*, updated 16 January 2016, at https://www.abc.net.au/news/2014-01-16/former-abc-journalist-describes-south-sudan-situation/5201234.

Shelton, Tracey, and Bill Birtles, 'Australians in Wuhan fleeing coronavirus evacuate on flight bound for WA and then Christmas Island', *ABC News*, updated 3 February 2020, at https://www.abc.net.au/news/2020-02-03/coronavirus-escaping-australians-evacuated-from-wuhan-on-flight/11922638.

Smart, Philip, 'Australian Defence Force in Vanuatu relief missions', *Australian Defence Magazine*, updated 18 March 2015, at https://www.australiandefence.com.au/news/australian-defence-force-in-vanuatu-relief-missions.

Smoleniec, Bethan, 'Qantas jet ready to evacuate Australians from quarantined cruise ship in Japan', *SBS News*, updated 18 February 2020, at https://www.sbs.com.au/news/article/qantas-jet-ready-to-evacuate-australians-from-quarantined-cruise-ship-in-japan/qmj9eetam.

'Some Bali bombing victims may never be identified,' *The Age*, updated 15 October 2002, at https://www.theage.com.au/national/some-bali-bombing-victims-may-never-be-identified-20021015-gduoxn.html.

'South Sudan: Nowhere safe: Civilians under attack in South Sudan', *Amnesty International*, updated 8 May 2014, at https://www.amnesty.org/en/documents/afr65/003/2014/en/.

Spector, Ronald H, 'Vietnam War', *Encyclopaedia Britannica*, updated 14 February 2020, at https://www.britannica.com/event/Vietnam-War.

'St George cut off by flood waters', *ABC News*, updated 6 February 2012, at https://www.abc.net.au/news/2012-02-06/st-george-cut-off-by-flood-waters/3812712.

'Travellers stuck in Peru, Argentina and South Africa amid coronavirus pandemic to get Qantas flights', *ABC News*, updated 10 April 2020, at https://www.abc.net.au/news/2020-04-09/coronavirus-rescue-flights-to-bring-australians-home-peru/12136946.

'Tropical Cyclone Winston – support to Fiji', *Department of Foreign Affairs and Trade*, n. d., at https://www.dfat.gov.au/crisis-hub/tropical-cyclone-winston-support-to-fiji.

'Victims' bodies repatriated after Indonesia crash', *ABC News*, updated 14 March 2007, at https://www.abc.net.au/news/2007-03-14/victims-bodies-repatriated-after-indonesia-crash/2216480.

Vogan, Mark, 'A Look Back: Winter of 1946–47', *MarkVoganWeather.com*, updated 12 December 2015, at http://www.markvoganweather.com/2015/12/12/a-look-back-winter-of-1946-47/.

Walden, Max, and Catherine Graue, 'Australian aid to help Cyclone Harold relief efforts as COVID-19 frustrates response', *ABC News*, updated 10 April 2020, at https://www.abc.net.au/news/2020-04-10/adf-plane-to-deliver-relief-to-vanuatu-after-cyclone-harold/12140456.

Waldron, Greg, 'Boeing C-17 steps up in Japan relief effort', *FlightGlobal*, updated 7 April 2011, at https://www.flightglobal.com/pictures-boeing-c-17-steps-up-in-japan-relief-effort/99274.article.

Westphalen, Neil, 'Humanitarian Aid/Disaster Relief (HA/DR) in the Australian Defence Force: Health aspects', *Journal of Military and Veterans' Health*, updated 21 March 2024, at https://jmvh.org/article/humanitarian-aid-disaster-relief-ha-dr-in-the-australian-defence-force-health-aspects/.

'When the Navy sailed to cyclone-ravaged Darwin', *National Archives of Australia*, updated 14 January 2020, at https://www.naa.gov.au/blog/when-navy-sailed-cyclone-ravaged-darwin.

'Why humanitarian aid is a powerful foreign policy strategy', *Big Think*, updated 20 July 2018, at https://bigthink.com/politics-current-affairs/why-humanitarian-aid-is-a-powerful-foreign-policy-strategy/.

Yeo, Mike, 'Defence clarifies reason behind delayed Vanuatu aid shipment (with graphical explainer)', *Asia–Pacific Defence Reporter*, updated 16 April 2020, at https://asiapacificdefencereporter.com/defence-clarifies-reasons-behind-delayed-vanuatu-aid-shipment-with-apdrs-map-explainer/.

ENDNOTES

Prologue

1 Bingo is a pre-calculated fuel state at which point the aircraft must immediately recover to an airfield or carrier.

2 Horst Ellenberger, 'Interrupted Journey', *ABS Magazine*, August 1997; Tony McCormack, email to author, 21 June 2023; Tony McCormack, email to author, 26 April 2024.

Introduction

1 Neil Westphalen, 'Humanitarian Aid/Disaster Relief (HA/DR) in the Australian Defence Force: Health aspects', *Journal of Military and Veterans' Health*, updated 21 March 2024, at https://jmvh.org/article/humanitarian-aid-disaster-relief-ha-dr-in-the-australian-defence-force-health-aspects/.

2 Jeff Roquen, 'International law and "humanity" in the making and unmaking of European solidarity, 1830–1915', *European Review of History: Revue europeenne d'histoire*, 2017, 24:6, p. 891.

3 Ministry of Defence, *Joint Doctrine Publication 3-52—Disaster Relief Operations Overseas: the Military Contribution*, 3rd edn, Development, Concepts and Doctrine Centre, Swindon, 2016, p. 10; Vanessa Newby, 'ANZUS cooperation in humanitarian assistance and disaster response in the Asia-Pacific: ships in the night?', *Australian Journal of International Affairs*, 2020, 74:1, p. 73.

4 Commonwealth of Australia, *Campaigns and Operations*, 3rd edn, Doctrine Directorate, Canberra, 2023, p. 42.

5 Commonwealth of Australia, *Stabilisation and Humanitarian Operations*, Doctrine Directorate, Canberra, 2023, p. 64.

6 Parliament of the Commonwealth of Australia, *Review of the Defence Annual Report 2003–04*, Joint Standing Committee on Defence, Foreign Affairs and Trade, Canberra, 2005, p. 47.

7 Ibid., p. 59.

8 Parliament of the Commonwealth of Australia, *Review of the Defence Annual Report 2003–04*, Joint Standing Committee on Defence, Foreign Affairs and Trade, Canberra, 2005, p. 36.

9 'Humanitarian and Relief Operations', p. 54.

10 Ibid., p. 55.

11 Parliament of the Commonwealth of Australia, *Review of the Defence Annual Report 2003–04*, Joint Standing Committee on Defence, Foreign Affairs and Trade, Canberra, 2005, p. 39.

12 Westphalen, 'Humanitarian Aid/Disaster Relief (HA/DR) in the Australian Defence Force'.

13 Newby, 'ANZUS cooperation in humanitarian assistance and disaster response in the Asia-Pacific'.

14 Commonwealth of Australia, *Stabilisation and Humanitarian Operations*, p. 1.

15 Westphalen, 'Humanitarian Aid/Disaster Relief (HA/DR) in the Australian Defence Force'.

16 Newby, 'ANZUS cooperation in humanitarian assistance and disaster response in the Asia-Pacific', p. 82.

17 'Humanitarian and Relief Operations', p. 52.

18 Commonwealth of Australia, *ADF Air Power*, Air and Space Power Centre, Canberra, 2023, p. 14

19 Commonwealth of Australia, *Australian Air Publication 1000–D—The Air Power Manual*, 6th edn, Air Power Development Centre, Canberra, 2013, p. 113.

20 Commonwealth of Australia, *Australian Maritime Doctrine: RAN Doctrine 1*, Sea Power Centre – Australia, Canberra, 2010, p. 86.

21 Ibid., p. 110.

22 'Humanitarian and Relief Operations', p. 53.

23 Tony McCormack, 'Air Power in Disaster Relief: The Role of the Royal Australian Air Force in Australia's Response to the 2011 Japanese Earthquake and Tsunami', Canberra, 31 July 2014.

Part I

1 Doina Anca Cretu, 'Nationalizing international relief: Romanian responses to American aid for children in the Great War era', *European Review of History: Revue europeenne d'histoire*, 2020, 27:1–2, p. 41.

2 Deon V Canyon, Benjamin J Ryan, and Frederick M Burkle, 'Military Provision of Humanitarian Assistance and Disaster Relief in Non-Conflict Crises', *Journal of Homeland Security and Emergency Management*, 2017, 17:45.

3 Friederike Kind-Kovács, 'The Great War, the child's body and the American Red Cross', *European Review of History: Revue européenne d'histoire*, 2016, 23:1–2, p. 34.

4 Ibid., p. 56.

5 Cretu, 'Nationalizing international relief', pp. 3–4.

6 Steven Bullard, *In Their Time of Need: Australia's overseas emergency relief operations, 1918–2006*, Cambridge University Press, Cambridge, 2017, p. 24.

7 Pierre Fuller, 'Decentring international and institutional famine relief in late nineteenth-century China: in search of the local', *European Review of History: Revue europeenne d'histoire*, 2015, 22:6, p. 884.

8 Tehila Sasson, and James Vernon, 'Practising the British way of famine: technologies of relief, 1770–1985', *European Review of History: Revue europeenne d'histoire*, 2015, 22:6, p. 861.

9 Ibid.

10 Roquen, 'International law and "humanity" in the making and unmaking of European solidarity, 1830–1915'.

11 Ibid.

12 Ibid.

13 Ibid.

14 Frederick C Cuny, 'Use of the Military in Humanitarian relief', *Frontline*, updated November 1989, at https://www.pbs.org/wgbh/pages/frontline/shows/cuny/laptop/humanrelief.html#:~:text=To%20date%2C%20the%20most%20common,of%20the%20Red%20Cross%20(ICRC).

15 Cretu, 'Nationalizing international relief', p. 2.

16 Ibid.

17 Patrick Merziger, 'The "radical humanism" of "Cap Anamur"/"German Emergency Doctors" in the 1980s: a turning point for the idea, practice and policy of humanitarian aid', *European Review of History: Revue européenne d'histoire*, 2016, 23:1–2, p. 172.

18 'Humanitarian preparedness and response', *Department of Foreign Affairs and Trade*, n. d., at https://www.dfat.gov.au/development/topics/development-issues/building-resilience/humanitarian-preparedness-and-response.

19 Joint Chiefs of Staff, *Joint Publication 3-29—Foreign Humanitarian Assistance*, Joint Force Development, Washington, 2019, p. vii.

20 'Humanitarian preparedness and response'.

21 Percy Spender, 'International affairs', Parliament of Australia, Canberra, 9 March 1950.

22 'Humanitarian preparedness and response'.

23 Jacinta O'Hagan, 'Australia and the promise and the perils of humanitarian diplomacy', *Australian Journal of International Affairs*, 2016, 70:6, p. 663.

24 Newby, 'ANZUS cooperation in humanitarian assistance and disaster response in the Asia-Pacific', p. 82.

25 'Humanitarian preparedness and response'.

26 Newby, 'ANZUS cooperation in humanitarian assistance and disaster response in the Asia-Pacific', pp. 79, 81–2.

27 'Why humanitarian aid is a powerful foreign policy strategy', *Big Think*, updated 20 July 2018, at https://bigthink.com/politics-current-affairs/why-humanitarian-aid-is-a-powerful-foreign-policy-strategy/.

28 Ministry of Defence, *Disaster Relief Operations Overseas*, p. 13.

29 'Why humanitarian aid is a powerful foreign policy strategy'.

30 Ibid.

31 Ibid.

32 Ibid.

33 Ministry of Defence, *Disaster Relief Operations Overseas*, p. 13.

34 O'Hagan, 'Australia and the promise and the perils of humanitarian diplomacy', p. 661.

35 'Humanitarian Principles', United Nations Office for the Coordination of Humanitarian Affairs, New York, 2022, at https://www.unocha.org/publications/report/world/ocha-message-humanitarian-principles-enar, p. 2.

36 Ibid.

37 Ibid. p. 1.
38 Cuny, 'Use of the Military in Humanitarian relief'.
39 Kind-Kovács, 'The Great War, the child's body and the American Red Cross', p. 35.
40 Ibid., p. 33.
41 Silvia Salvatici, '"Fighters without guns": humanitarianism and military action in the aftermath of the Second World War', *European Review of History: Revue europeenne d'histoire*, 2018, 25:6, p. 970.
42 Merziger, 'The "radical humanism" of "Cap Anamur"/"German Emergency Doctors" in the 1980s', p. 171; Cuny, 'Use of the Military in Humanitarian relief'.
43 Canyon, et al., 'Military Provision of Humanitarian Assistance and Disaster Relief in Non-Conflict Crises', p. 2.
44 Ibid.
45 Ibid., p. 1.
46 Ministry of Defence, *Disaster Relief Operations Overseas*, p. 10; Newby, 'ANZUS cooperation in humanitarian assistance and disaster response in the Asia-Pacific', p. 73.
47 Ministry of Defence, *Disaster Relief Operations Overseas*, pp. 11, 15, 19.
48 North Atlantic Treaty Organization, *Allied Joint Doctrine for the Military Contribution to Humanitarian Assistance*, NATO Standardization Office, Brussels, 2015, p. 1.5.
49 Ibid., p. IX.
50 'Humanitarian Principles', p. 1.
51 Canyon, et al., 'Military Provision of Humanitarian Assistance and Disaster Relief in Non-Conflict Crises', p. 2.

Part II: Chapter 1

1 Nathaniel D Bastian, et al, 'Multi-criteria logistics modeling for military humanitarian assistance and disaster relief aerial delivery operations', *Springer*, 2014, 10, p. 922.
2 Bullard, *In Their Time of Need*, p. 91.
3 Ibid., p. 88.
4 Bullard, *In Their Time of Need*, p. 155.
5 'Providing COVID-19 assistance to Samoa and Solomon Islands', *Air Force News*, 17 February 2022, p. 9.
6 Ibid.
7 Natsumi Penberthy, 'On this day in history: 2004 Boxing Day tsunami', *Australian Geographic*, updated 18 December 2014, at https://www.australiangeographic.com.au/blogs/on-this-day/2014/12/on-this-day-in-history-boxing-day-tsunami/.
8 'Indian Ocean tsunami', *Department of Foreign Affairs and Trade*, updated 19 December 2014, at https://www.dfat.gov.au/news/news/Pages/indian-ocean-tsunami.
9 'Thank you from Tonga', *Air Force News*, 31 March 2022, p. 7.
10 Ibid.
11 Ibid.
12 Elosegui Guerra, email to author, 18 May 2023.
13 Ibid.
14 'Australian support to Ukraine', *Air Force News*, 17 March 2022, p. 3; 'First PMVs to Ukraine', *Air Force News*, 14 April 2022, p. 4.
15 Kathryn Reid, '2011 Japan earthquake and tsunami: Facts, FAQs, and how to help', *World Vision*, updated 7 May 2019, at https://www.worldvision.org/disaster-relief-news-stories/2011-japan-earthquake-and-tsunami-facts#:~:text=Fast%20facts%3A%202011%20Japan%20earthquake%20and%20tsunami,-The%20T-%C5%8Dhoku%20earthquake&text=At%20%24360%20billion%2C%20the%20earthquake,from%20drowning%20during%20the%20tsunami; 'Humanitarian support', *Royal Australian Air Force*, n. d., at https://www.airforce.gov.au/our-work/humanitarian-support.
16 Greg Waldron, 'Boeing C-17 steps up in Japan relief effort', *FlightGlobal*, updated 7 April 2011, at https://www.flightglobal.com/pictures-boeing-c-17-steps-up-in-japan-relief-effort/99274.article.
17 Tony McCormack, email to author, 22 May 2023.
18 Ibid.

19 'Tropical Cyclone Winston – support to Fiji', *Department of Foreign Affairs and Trade*, n. d., at https://www.dfat.gov.au/crisis-hub/tropical-cyclone-winston-support-to-fiji.

20 Ibid.

21 'Operation Fiji Assist widens – LHD deployed,' *Australian Defence Magazine*, updated 24 February 2016, at https://www.australiandefence.com.au/news/operation-fiji-assist-widens-lhd-deployed.

22 Ibid.

23 Zoe Griffyn, 'Taipans deliver vital aid', *Army News*, 4 February 2021, p. 10.

24 Ibid.

25 Bruce Chalmers, 'Warm greeting for a timely delivery', *Air Force News*, 16 March 2023, p. 3.

26 Ibid.

27 Jace Hutchison, email to author, 25 June 2023.

28 Ibid.

29 Mike Yeo, 'Defence clarifies reason behind delayed Vanuatu aid shipment (with graphical explainer)', *Asia–Pacific Defence Reporter*, updated 16 April 2020, at https://asiapacificdefencereporter.com/defence-clarifies-reasons-behind-delayed-vanuatu-aid-shipment-with-apdrs-map-explainer/; Max Walden and Catherine Graue, 'Australian aid to help Cyclone Harold relief efforts as COVID-19 frustrates response', *ABC News*, updated 10 April 2020, at https://www.abc.net.au/news/2020-04-10/adf-plane-to-deliver-relief-to-vanuatu-after-cyclone-harold/12140456.

30 Clarice Hurren, 'Loads of relief for neighbours in crisis', *Air Force News*, 30 April 2020, p. 7.

31 'Providing COVID-19 assistance to Samoa and Solomon Islands'.

32 Ibid.

33 Stuart Wheal, email to author, 20 May 2023.

34 Ibid.

35 Sam Schmidt, email to author, 16 June 2023.

36 Ibid.

37 'Berlin Airlift', *Digger History*, n. d., at http://www.diggerhistory.info/pages-battles/berlin-airlift.htm.

38 Ibid.

39 Ibid.

40 Bullard, *In Their Time of Need*, p. 480.

41 'Infographic: Nepal earthquake – Australian Government humanitarian response', *Department of Foreign Affairs and Trade*, updated 19 December 2019, at https://www.dfat.gov.au/news/news/Pages/nepal-earthquake-australian-government-humanitarian-response#:~:text=Infographic%3A%20Nepal%20earthquake%20%2D%20Australian%20Government%20humanitarian%20response,-19%20December%202019&text=The%20Australian%20Government%20has%20provided,million%20in%20lifesaving%20humanitarian%20support.

42 'Operation NEPAL ASSIST 2015', *Department of Defence*, n. d., at https://www.airforce.gov.au/about-us/history/our-journey/operation-nepal-assist#:~:text=Following%20a%20devastating%20earthquake%20on,other%20foreign%20nationals%20to%20Thailand; Andrew Greene, 'Nepal earthquake: Aid, RAAF medical evacuation teams on way to Nepal but ADF aircraft still unable to land', *ABC News*, updated 29 April 2015, at https://www.abc.net.au/news/2015-04-29/australian-defence-aircraft-still-unable-to-land-in-nepal/6430802.

43 Ibid.

44 'South Sudan: Nowhere safe: Civilians under attack in South Sudan', *Amnesty International*, updated 8 May 2014, at https://www.amnesty.org/en/documents/afr65/003/2014/en/.

45 'Humanitarian support'.

46 Irene Scott, 'South Sudan crisis: Former ABC journalist Irene Scott travels with RAAF crew on relief mission', *ABC News*, updated 16 January 2016, at https://www.abc.net.au/news/2014-01-16/former-abc-journalist-describes-south-sudan-situation/5201234.

47 'Cyclone Tracy, 1974', *Knowledge Hub*, n. d., at https://knowledge.aidr.org.au/resources/cyclone-cyclone-tracy-darwin-1974/.

48 'Disaster relief – Cyclone Tracy and Tasman Bridge', *Sea Power Centre Australia*, updated December 2004, at https://www.navy.gov.au/history/feature-histories/disaster-relief-cyclone-tracy-and-tasman-bridge#:~:text=Between%201%20and%2030%20January,commercial%20buildings%20and%20recreational%20facilities.

49 Patrick Barkham and Adam Gabbatt, 'Cyclone Yasi strikes North Queensland', *The Guardian*, updated 3 February 2011, at https://www.theguardian.com/world/2011/feb/02/cyclone-yasi-north-queensland.

50 'Humanitarian support'.

51 Ibid.

52 'That's a wrap for OP Flood Assist', *Air Force News*, 2 March 2023, p. 2.

53 Ibid.

54 Shaunn Segon, email to author, 8 June 2023.

55 Ibid.

56 Bullard, *In Their Time of Need*, p. 158.

57 'Bali bombings', *National Museum Australia*, n. d., at https://www.nma.gov.au/defining-moments/resources/bali-bombings; Qantas Airways Limited, *2003 Qantas Annual Report*, Qantas Airways Limited, Mascot, 2005, p. 24.

58 'Qantas Milestones and Transactions', *Qantas*, updated November 2015, at https://investor.qantas.com/home/?page=milestones-and-transactions.

59 Mark Vogan, 'A LOOK BACK: Winter of 1946-47', *MarkVoganWeather.com*, updated 12 December 2015, at http://www.markvoganweather.com/2015/12/12/a-look-back-winter-of-1946-47/.

60 Kathy Marks, 'Qantas celebrates 60 years of the "Kangaroo Route"', *The Independent*, updated 30 November 2007, at https://www.independent.co.uk/news/world/australasia/qantas-celebrates-60-years-of-the-kangaroo-route-761078.html.

61 Stephen Dziedzic, 'About 900 Australians stuck in COVID-hit India and wanting to return now listed as "vulnerable", High Commissioner says', *ABC News*, updated 6 May 2021, at https://www.abc.net.au/news/2021-05-05/australians-health-high-commission-india-supplies-covid-19/100117620.

62 Ibid.

63 '2019–2020 Australian Bushfires', *Center for Disaster Philanthropy*, updated 17 February 2020, at https://disasterphilanthropy.org/disasters/2019-australian-wildfires/#:~:text=Donations%20to%20the%20CDP%20Global,three%2Dyear%20bushfire%20recovery%20program.

64 Bastian, et al., 'Multi-criteria logistics modeling for military humanitarian assistance and disaster relief aerial delivery operations', pp. 922–3.

65 Eric E Geiselman, et al., 'Airdrop guidance display format for precision airdrop application on an auxiliary display equipped aircraft', *The International Journal of Aviation Psychology*, 2015, 25:3–4, p. 141.

66 Ibid., p. 142; 'RAAF advances airdrop capability', *Australian Defence Magazine*, updated 26 August 2015, at https://www.australiandefence.com.au/news/raaf-advances-airdrop-capability#:~:text=The%20RAAF%20has%20advanced%20its,zone%20by%20using%20steerable%20parachutes.

67 Ibid.

68 Ibid.

69 Ibid.

70 Bastian, et al., 'Multi-criteria logistics modeling for military humanitarian assistance and disaster relief aerial delivery operations', p. 922.

71 '4 years ago: the genocide against the Yazidis in northern Iraq (August 3, 2014)', *Gesellschaft für bedrohte Völker*, updated 8 February 2018, at https://www.gfbv.de/en/news/4-years-ago-the-genocide-against-the-yazidis-in-northern-iraq-august-3-2014-9323/.

72 Valeria Cetorelli, et al., 'ISIS' Yazidi Genocide: Demographic Evidence of the Killings and Kidnappings', *Foreign Affairs*, updated 8 June 2017, at https://www.foreignaffairs.com/articles/syria/2017-06-08/isis-yazidi-genocide.

73 'Iraq crisis: Australian plane drops humanitarian aid into Amerli residents under siege by Islamic State militants', *ABC News*, updated 31 August 2014, at https://www.abc.net.au/news/2014-08-31/australian-planes-drop-humanitarian-aid-into-iraq/5708636.

74 Commonwealth of Australia, 'Stabilisation and Humanitarian Operations', p. 67.

75 Commonwealth of Australia, *ADF Air Power*, p. 18.

Part II: Chapter 2

1 Ronald H Spector, 'Vietnam War', *Encyclopaedia Britannica*, updated 14 February 2020, at https://www.britannica.com/event/Vietnam-War.

2 'Rescue flight brings Vietnamese orphans out of Saigon', Anzac Portal, updated 16 November 2022, at https://anzacportal.dva.gov.au/stories/australians-wartime/rescue-flight-brings-vietnamese-orphans-out-saigon; 'Operation Babylift', Anzac Portal, n. d., at https://anzacportal.dva.gov.au/wars-and-missions/vietnam-war-1962-1975/royal-australian-air-force/raaf-1975#1.

3 'Rescue flight brings Vietnamese orphans out of Saigon'.

4 Graham O'Brien, *Always There: A History of Air Force Combat Support*, Air Power Development Centre, Canberra, 2009, p. 73.

5 Andrew Nachemson, 'Was Cambodia Ever Really a Democracy?', *The Diplomat*, updated 4 July 2019, at https://thediplomat.com/2019/07/was-cambodia-ever-really-a-democracy/; O'Brien, *Always There: A History of Air Force Combat Support*, p. 86.

6 Ibid.

7 Ibid.

8 'ADF: past operations in Timor-Leste (East Timor)', *Nautilus Institute*, n. d., at https://nautilus.org/publications/books/australian-forces-abroad/east-timor/adf-past-operations-in-timor-leste-east-timor/.

9 O'Brien, *Always There: A History of Air Force Combat Support*, p. 194.

10 Kathryn Reid, '2015 Cyclone Pam: Facts, FAQs, and how to help', *World Vision*, updated 3 July 2018, at https://www.worldvision.org/disaster-relief-news-stories/2015-vanuatu-cyclone-pam-facts#:~:text=Cyclone%20Pam%20struck%20Vanuatu%20as,affected%20areas%20were%20wiped%20out; Brad Richardson, 'Help to return home', *Air Force News*, 26 March 2015, p. 2; Philip Smart, 'Australian Defence Force in Vanuatu relief missions', *Australian Defence Magazine*, updated 18 March 2015, at https://www.australiandefence.com.au/news/australian-defence-force-in-vanuatu-relief-missions.

11 Ibid.

12 Siobhan Heanue, 'Nepal earthquake: First Australians evacuated from Kathmandu on board RAAF transport planes', *ABC News*, updated 1 May 2015, at https://www.abc.net.au/news/2015-05-01/nepal-aid-reaches-earthquake-zone-australians-evacuated/6436476.

13 Bullard, *In Their Time of Need*, p. 482; '817 Squadron History', *Royal Australian Navy*, n. d., at https://www.navy.gov.au/history/squadron-histories/817-squadron-history.

14 Ibid., p. 221; Ibid., p. 222; 'Operation Ramp [electronic resource]', *Australian War Memorial*, n. d., at https://www.awm.gov.au/collection/LIB100011631; 'Operation Ramp', *Migrants in Countries in Crisis*, n. d., at https://micicinitiative.iom.int/operation-ramp-0.

15 '2006: Lebanon war', BBC News, updated 6 May 2008, at http://news.bbc.co.uk/2/hi/middle_east/7381389.stm.

16 O'Brien, *Always There: A History of Air Force Combat Support*, p. 222.

17 Kevin Auld, email to author, 14 September 2023.

18 Ibid.

19 Angus Campbell, 'Operations end in Afghanistan', *Air Force News*, 5 August 2021, p. 2; Angus Campbell, 'Thank you to all ADF members', *Air Force News*, 2 September 2021, p. 2; Andrew Ragless, 'Compassion and pride in historic airlift', *Air Force News*, 16 September 2021, pp. 2–3.

20 Ibid.

21 Ellen Whinnett, 'Operation Sudan Airlift', *The Weekend Australian*, 20–21 May 2023, p. 39; Matthew Doran, 'RAAF rescue mission evacuates 36 Australians and their family members from Sudan', *ABC News*, updated 3 May 2023, at https://www.abc.net.au/news/2023-05-03/australian-rescue-mission-flight-out-of-sudan/102295460.

22 Ibid.

23 Jacquelyn Nelson, email to author, 3 July 2023.

24 Ibid.

25 Bullard, *In Their Time of Need*, p. 482.

26 'Cyclone Tracy, 1974'.

27 Ibid.

28 'Spartans play role in NT flood evacuations', *Air Force News*, 16 March 2023, p. 5; Rob Hodgson, 'RAAF brings relief after the rain', *Air Force News*, 30 March 2023, p. 6.

29 Hodgson, 'RAAF brings relief after the rain'.

30 'Air Mobility Group', *Royal Australian Air Force*, n. d., at https://www.airforce.gov.au/about-us/hq-air-command/air-mobility-group.

31 Michael Serenc, 'Answering the call: RAAF responds with Yasi Assist', *Australian Aviation*, April 2011, pp. 60–1.

32 'Humanitarian support'; 'St George cut off by flood waters', *ABC News*, updated 6 February 2012, at https://www.abc.net.au/news/2012-02-06/st-george-cut-off-by-flood-waters/3812712.

33 Geoff Long, 'Ferrying families to safety', *Air Force News*, 2 February 2023, p. 3.

34 Ibid.

35 Deniele Oehm, email to author, 1 June 2023.

36 Ibid.

37 Matt O'Sullivan, 'Virgin in bid to unseat Qantas as Australia's chief airline for "rescue" flights', *The Sydney Morning Herald*, updated 13 December 2013, at https://www.smh.com.au/business/virgin-in-bid-to-unseat-qantas-as-australias-chief-airline-for-rescue-flights-20131212-2za5c.html.

38 'Qantas Milestones and Transactions'.

39 Qantas Airways Limited, *2003 Qantas Annual Report.*

40 'Egypt Uprising of 2011', *Encyclopaedia Britannica*, n. d., at https://www.britannica.com/event/Egypt-Uprising-of-2011.

41 Ibid.

42 'Qantas Milestones and Transactions'.

43 'Qantas offers free flights for Aussies in Egypt', *ABC News*, updated 2 February 2011, at https://www.abc.net.au/news/2011-02-02/qantas-offers-free-flights-for-aussies-in-egypt/1927462.

44 'Cyclone Tracy', *Library & Archives NT*, n. d., at https://lant.nt.gov.au/explore-nt-history/cyclone-tracy; 'Our history', *Qantas*, n. d., at https://www.qantas.com/au/en/about-us/our-company/our-history.html; 'Qantas Milestones and Transactions'.

45 Frances Bell and Evelyn Manfield, 'Passengers on coronavirus evacuation flight from Wuhan land on Christmas Island', *ABC News*, updated 4 February 2020, at https://www.abc.net.au/news/2020-02-03/coronavirus-wuhan-evacuation-flight-reaches-wa-christmas-island/11923324; Bethan Smoleniec, 'Qantas jet ready to evacuate Australians from quarantined cruise ship in Japan', *SBS News*, updated 18 February 2020, at https://www.sbs.com.au/news/article/qantas-jet-ready-to-evacuate-australians-from-quarantined-cruise-ship-in-japan/qmj9eetam; 'Travellers stuck in Peru, Argentina and South Africa amid coronavirus pandemic to get Qantas flights', *ABC News*, updated 10 April 2020, at https://www.abc.net.au/news/2020-04-09/coronavirus-rescue-flights-to-bring-australians-home-peru/12136946; 'Coronavirus rescue flights secured for Australians stranded in Peru, Argentina and South Africa', *SBS News*, updated 10 April 2020, at https://www.sbs.com.au/news/article/coronavirus-rescue-flights-secured-for-australians-stranded-in-peru-argentina-and-south-africa/sfd3fsi61.

46 'Rescue flight brings Vietnamese orphans out of Saigon'.

47 Ibid.

48 Ibid.

49 'Country profile – Vietnam', *Department of Home Affairs*, updated 22 July 2020, at https://www.homeaffairs.gov.au/research-and-statistics/statistics/country-profiles/profiles/vietnam.

Part II: Chapter 3

1 Tony McCormack, 21 June 2023.

2 Ibid; Ellenberger, 'Interrupted Journey'.

3 Bullard, *In Their Time of Need*, p. 239.

4 'Flood of support', *Air Force News*, 17 March 2022, pp. 4–5.

5 Roger McCutcheon, email to author, 15 June 2023.

6 Ibid.

7 'Humanitarian support'.

8 Craig Heap, email to author, 30 June 2023.

9 Ibid.

10 Cale Barnes, email to author, 20 June 2023.

11 RAAF Base Learmonth is one of the RAAF's three 'bare bases' which are maintained by a small number of caretaker personnel and are used almost solely during military exercises or operations.

12 Barnes.

13 'MH17 Ukraine plane crash: What we know', *BBC News*, updated 26 February 2020, at https://www.bbc.com/news/world-europe-28357880.

14 'AirAsia QZ8501: Search resumes for missing flight after anxious relatives spend night in crisis centre', *ABC News*, updated 29 December 2014, at https://www.abc.net.au/news/2014-12-29/airasia-flight-qz8501-search-to-resume/5990800.

15 'Humanitarian support'.

16 Ibid.

17 Bullard, *In Their Time of Need*, p. 88.

18 Eamon Hamilton, 'Analysts aided by live streaming', *Air Force News*, 3 February 2022, p. 3.

19 Ibid.

20 'Victims' bodies repatriated after Indonesia crash', *ABC News*, updated 14 March 2007, at https://www.abc.net.au/news/2007-03-14/victims-bodies-repatriated-after-indonesia-crash/2216480; Millar, Paul, 'Kokoda crash victims arrive home', *The Sydney Morning Herald*, updated 26 August 2009, at https://www.smh.com.au/national/kokoda-crash-victims-arrive-home-20090826-eyyc.html.

21 'Humanitarian support'.

22 Ibid.

23 'MH17 airbridge to Ukraine "smashing it"', *SBS News*, updated 31 July 2014, at https://www.sbs.com.au/news/article/mh17-airbridge-to-ukraine-smashing-it/l89pd9u1q.

24 'Some Bali bombing victims may never be identified,' *The Age*, updated 15 October 2002, at https://www.theage.com.au/national/some-bali-bombing-victims-may-never-be-identified-20021015-gduoxn.html; Qantas Airways Limited, *2003 Qantas Annual Report*.

Part II: Chapter 4

1 'Indian Ocean tsunami'; 'Australia's response to the Indian Ocean Tsunami: Report for the Period Ending 30 June 2005', *Parliament of Australia*, n. d., at https://www.dfat.gov.au/about-us/publications/Pages/australia-s-response-to-the-indian-ocean-tsunami-report-for-the-period-ending-30-june-2005.

2 Ted Aljibe, 'Philippines: five years after Typhoon Haiyan', *The Guardian*, updated 6 November 2018, at https://www.theguardian.com/artanddesign/2018/nov/06/philippines-five-years-after-typhoon-haiyan.

3 O'Hagan, 'Australia and the promise and the perils of humanitarian diplomacy', p. 663; Mark di Stefano, and Stephen McDonell, 'Typhoon Haiyan: Australian emergency medical team heads for Philippines', *ABC News*, updated 13 November 2013, at https://www.abc.net.au/news/2013-11-13/raaf-aircraft-prepare-to-fly-to-philippines-medical-team-typhoo/5088470.

4 Ibid.

5 Ibid; 'Providing COVID-19 assistance to Samoa and Solomon Islands'; Gordon Carr-Gregg, 'Big lift for Pacific friend', *Air Force News*, 5 August 2021, p. 3.

6 Jessica Aldred, 'Together for Tassie', *Air Force News*, 30 April 2020, p. 7.

7 Ibid.

8 Cameron Brockel, email to author, 22 May 2023.

9 Ibid.

10 Bullard, *In Their Time of Need*, p. 482.

11 Ibid.

12 'Australia doubles NZ quake help', *ABC News*, updated 22 February 2011, at https://www.abc.net.au/news/2011-02-22/australia-doubles-nz-quake-help/1953726.

13 'Air Mobility Group'; 'Australia doubles NZ quake help'.

14 Ibid.

15 Dean Squire, 'Help ferried to quake zone', *Air Force News*, 16 February 2023, p. 5.

16 Ibid.

17 McCormack, 'Air Power in Disaster Relief'.

18 Ibid.

19 'Devastated survivor describes Tongan ferry tragedy', *The Sydney Morning Herald*, updated 8 August 2009, at https://www.smh.com.au/world/devastated-survivor-describes-tongan-ferry-tragedy-20090808-edeo.html.

20 Michael Brooks, 'Crash Aid', *Air Force News*, 20 August 2009, p. 1–2.

21 Ibid.

22 Scott Broughton, email to author, 24 July 2023.

23 Ibid.

24 Commonwealth of Australia, *ADF Air Power*, p. 23.

25 'ADF moves to support fire crews', *Australian Defence Magazine*, updated 12 November 2019, at https://www.australiandefence.com.au/news/adf-moves-to-support-fire-crews; Robert Dougherty, 'Fire and Rescue NSW firefighters are being transported by Royal Australian Air Force planes to help battle the South Coast fires', *Port News*, updated 6 January 2020, at https://www.portnews.com.au/story/6567808/mid-north-coast-firefighters-deployed-to-nations-southern-frontline/.

26 Commonwealth of Australia, *ADF Air Power*, p. 23.

27 Kylie Jagiello, 'Caring for our people', *Air Force News*, 2 April 2020, p. 5.

28 Ibid.

29 Phil Baldoni, email to author, 23 May 2023.

30 Ibid.

31 David Weekley, email to author, 23 May 2023.

32 Ibid.

33 Bullard, *In Their Time of Need*, p. 25.

34 'Humanitarian support'.

35 Brooks, 'Crash Aid'.

36 Ibid.

37 'MH17 airbridge to Ukraine "smashing it"'.

38 'Humanitarian support'.

39 Martin Hadley, 'Neighbourly help with elections', *Air Force News*, 3 June 2022, p. 5.

40 Bullard, *In Their Time of Need*, p. 482.

41 'Australia's Response to Typhoon Yolanda', *Australian Embassy The Philippines*, n. d., at https://philippines.embassy.gov.au/mnla/TyphoonYolandaTyphoonYolanda.html#:~:text=Australia%27s%20Foreign%20Minister%20Julie%20Bishop,contribution%20to%20A%2430%20million.

42 Qantas Airways Limited, *2003 Qantas Annual Report.*

43 Qantas Airways Limited, *Qantas Annual Report 2005*, p. 30.

44 'Our community', *Qantas*, n. d., at https://www.qantas.com/au/en/qantas-group/acting-responsibly/our-community.html.

Part III

1 'Fit for the future: Priorities for Australia's humanitarian action', *Australian Council for International Development*, updated 17 February 2020, at https://acfid.asn.au/acfid-releases-guidance-for-the-development-of-a-disability-inclusion-policy-3-15/.

2 'Humanitarian preparedness and response'.

3 'Fit for the future: Priorities for Australia's humanitarian action', p. 8.

4 Ibid., p. 37; Newby, 'ANZUS cooperation in humanitarian assistance and disaster response in the Asia-Pacific', p. 73.

5 'Fit for the future: Priorities for Australia's humanitarian action', p. 33

6 Newby, 'ANZUS cooperation in humanitarian assistance and disaster response in the Asia-Pacific', p. 73.

7 'Humanitarian preparedness and response'.

8 Bullard, *In Their Time of Needs*, p. 30.

9 'Fit for the future: Priorities for Australia's humanitarian action', p. 8.

10 'Australia's Response to Typhoon Yolanda'.

11 Ibid.

12 Serenc, 'Answering the call: RAAF responds with Yasi Assist'.

13 Hamilton and Easton, 'Help home and away'.

14 Tracey Shelton and Bill Birtles, 'Australians in Wuhan fleeing coronavirus evacuate on flight bound for WA and then Christmas Island', *ABC News*, updated 3 February 2020, at https://www.abc.net.au/news/2020-02-03/coronavirus-escaping-australians-evacuated-from-wuhan-on-flight/11922638.

15 Ibid.

Conclusion

1 Richardson, 'Help to return home'.

INDEX